Curiosities Series

FLORIDA
Curiosities

Quirky Characters, Roadside Oddities & Other Offbeat Stuff

David Grimes and Tom Becnel

The
GlobePequot
Press

GUILFORD, CONNECTICUT

Cover design: Nancy Freeborn
Text design: Bill Brown
Layout: Deborah Nicolais
Maps: XNR Productions Inc. © The Globe Pequot Press
Photo credits: All photos are by the authors unless otherwise noted.

ISBN 0-7627-2365-3
Manufactured in the United States of America
First Edition/Third Printing

The prices and rates listed in this guidebook were confirmed at press time. We recommend, however, that you call establishments before traveling to obtain current information.

FLORIDA
Curiosities

Help Us Keep This Guide Up to Date

Every effort has been made by the authors and editors to make this guide as accurate and useful as possible. However, many things can change after a guide is published—establishments close, phone numbers change, facilities come under new management, etc.

We would love to hear from you concerning your experiences with this guide and how you feel it could be improved and kept up to date. While we may not be able to respond to all comments and suggestions, we'll take them to heart and we'll also make certain to share them with the author. Please send your comments and suggestions to the following address:

The Globe Pequot Press
Reader Response/Editorial Department
P.O. Box 480
Guilford, CT 06437

Or you may e-mail us at:

editorial@globe-pequot.com

Thanks for your input, and happy travels!

Contents

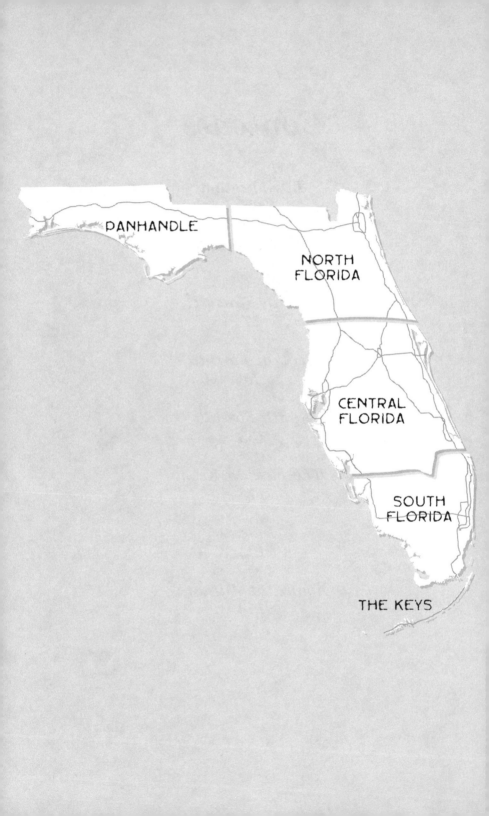

INTRODUCTION

lorida was a State of Confusion long before the 2000 presidential election. This is a place where tourists are told to go north if they want to visit the South. (The north and northwestern Florida counties are more like Alabama than Miami, which is more like South America than the United States.)

This is a state that many people believe begins and ends with Disney World and where the joke still circulates that any 7-Eleven built before 1985 qualifies as a historic building. Yet one of our more popular tourist destinations continues to be St. Augustine, a city founded fifty-five years before the Pilgrims landed at Plymouth Rock.

When people think of Florida they think of Mickey Mouse and orange juice. But Florida is also the biggest beef-producing state east of the Mississippi River. The sugar you dump into your coffee every morning probably comes from Florida, as does the houseplant on your desk. Most of Florida's more than sixteen million residents live within 15 miles of the coast and seldom venture into the interior of the state, a place of numberless lakes, oak and pine forests, gin-clear springs, and fragrant orange groves stretching from horizon to horizon.

In west central Florida, you're as likely to hear the Midwestern twang of a transplanted Michigander as you are a southern drawl. In south Florida, your grandmother from New Jersey is likely to be the Democrat and the young Cuban immigrant the Republican. (You will remember that the Republicans, who allegedly embrace family values, disapproved of sending Elian Gonzalez back to his father in Cuba and that the Democrats, who allegedly embrace civil liberties, were the ones who

No need for extra oxygen when visiting Florida's highest point. At 345
feet, this bump in the road in Lakewood, just below the Alabama state
line, is as high as it gets in the Sunshine State.

arranged for the "rescue" of the six-year-old boy at gunpoint.)

In the Keys, confusion has been raised to an art form. In Key West, drifters and developers drink in the same saloons Ernest Hemingway once frequented. At Hemingway's house, the six-toed cats drink from a urinal rescued from one of his watering holes. Some years ago, the mayor of Key West water-skied to Havana to protest the proposed closing of the Navy base. No one thought this was the least bit strange, and the Navy, perhaps realizing it was up against a superior force, decided to stay put.

Tourists who know nothing of Florida other than the theme parks near Orlando may be surprised by the state's size. It is just about the same distance to Chicago from Pensacola, in the Panhandle, as it is from Pensacola to Key West. If you like beaches, there are 663 miles of them to explore in Florida. If you like to fish, there are 1,197 miles of coastline.

Florida is also the place to go if you like to eat. Apalachicola is famous for its oysters, Indian River is famous for its oranges, and Clewiston, which calls itself "The Sweetest Town in America," is famous for its sugarcane. Elsewhere, there are mullet festivals, blue crab festivals, chili festivals, strawberry festivals, and . . . well, basically a festival for every type of food you can imagine.

This book is a guide to and a celebration of the unseen Florida, the quirky people, places, and things that give our state its character and charm. We'll meet the man responsible for kudzu, a woman who entertains children by dressing up as a skunk ape, and a ninety-one-year-old snake charmer. We'll visit the world's largest McDonald's, the Elian Gonzalez shrine, and a theater where Shakespeare is performed in the nude.

Do you like celebrations and festivals? We'll walk you through the Love Bug Festival, tell you how to dress up for the Redneck Parade, and explain the techniques used in the Worm Fiddling Festival.

After finishing the book, you might conclude that the 2000 election wasn't so abnormal after all.

PANHANDLE

THE PANHANDLE

THE ICE MAN COMETH
Apalachicola

I f you are able to live through a Florida summer without melting into a puddle of goo, you should give thanks to John Gorrie, the inventor of air conditioning.

There may be some inventions we appreciate more than air conditioning—beer springs immediately to mind—but they are hard to imagine when you've been working outdoors in August and take that first glorious step into an air-conditioned building.

How did people live in Florida before air conditioning? Moistly is probably the best answer.

In 1842 Gorrie, an Apalachicola medical doctor, invented refrigeration as the result of experiments to lower patients' fevers by cooling their hospital rooms. The scientific principle—heating a gas by compressing it, cooling it by sending it through radiating coils, and then expanding the gas to cool it further—is the same principle used in refrigerators and air-conditioners today.

The story is that Gorrie was trying to build a machine to cool hospital rooms, but the thing kept freezing up and spewing out ice. Although Gorrie was granted the first U.S. patent for mechanical refrigeration in 1851, he never profited from it. Willis Haviland Carrier, who is often credited with inventing air-conditioning even though he only modified Corrie's technology for commercial use sixty years later, made the money.

John Gorrie, the inventor of air conditioning, did more for Florida
tourism than Walt Disney. A small museum in Apalachicola honors this
dubious distinction.

Gorrie's contribution to Southern living was so monumental
that a museum was built in his honor in Apalachicola. Inside
the one-room building is a model of his invention, which is
really a primitive ice machine.

Gorrie, one of Apalachicola's pioneers, died there in 1855 at
the age of fifty-one. A middle school in Jacksonville is named
after him, and there is a statue of the inventor in the rotunda
of the Capitol in Washington, D.C.

Pretty cool, huh?

The John Gorrie Museum is located at 46 Sixth Street,
Apalachicola. The museum is open from 9:00 A.M. to 5:00 P.M.
Thursday through Monday. Admission is $1.00. Phone (850)
653–9347.

PARROTS THAT DON'T TALK BACK
Apalachicola

Not everyone in Apalachicola—or "Apalach" as it's known to the locals—fishes.

Joseph Moberly, a retired claims adjuster, carves things—big things—out of wood and displays them in his front yard at 202 Fourth Street. There's an 8-foot-tall sea captain in a bright yellow rain slicker with a red snapper in one hand and a fish net in the other. He's called Capt. Walt Shell in honor of Moberly's good buddy of the same name across the street. Next to the captain is a pair of tail-walking dolphins, and next to them is Moby, a colorful cigar-and-shot-glass-toting parrot named after his own parrot. (It doesn't pay to live close to or with Joe Moberly unless you want your likeness carved out of a cypress log and set out in the front yard for all the world to see.)

The wooden menagerie is added to and subtracted from on a regular basis. Moberly doesn't sell anything, but he occasionally gives a carving to a friend or relative. You'll also find his stuff lurking in downtown parks, and careful viewers of the movie *Coastlines* might have spotted several of his sculptures in the bar scenes.

A self-described "old fart," the sixty-eight-year-old says carving is a hobby that keeps him busy and helps him fend off depression. The whimsical nature of his sculptures certainly cheers up others in this hardworking town where most people's idea of art is a shrimp net or a pair of oyster tongs.

Moberly says the carvings take him a week to a week and a half to complete using a chain saw and other power equipment.

"A lot of people think I'm sitting on my front porch whittling these things with a knife," he says. "That's not true."

Joseph Moberly's house in Apalachicola is guarded by an interesting menagerie. Carved Indians and dolphins provide special security.

Moberly is a self-taught sculptor who gets his ideas from the library, other sculptors and, of all places, Wal-Mart.

"I'll buy a trinket at Wal-Mart, a little ceramic dog or something, and then I'll set it down in front of me and magnify it," he said.

So if you're walking by Moberly's house and get frightened by an 8-foot wooden dog tied up to the gate, you'll have Wal-Mart to blame.

SHUT UP AND SHUCK!
Apalachicola

Believe it or not, Apalachicola, the Oyster Capital of the state, had until recently only one raw bar. That's like Kansas City having only one steak house or Seattle only one Starbucks.

But it's true. If you wanted to tuck in to some plump, salty, freshly shucked oysters tonged a few hours earlier from Apalachicola Bay, the only game in town was Boss Oyster.

A second raw bar, Papa Joe's, opened a couple of years ago, but Boss Oyster is still viewed by many as The Place. They certainly shell out the shellfish, serving ninety-four tons in a typical year in a restaurant that seats 300, according to head chef "Big" Tim Strand.

While you're sitting on the open-air deck, trying to decide which one of the five varieties of hot sauce you want to sprinkle on your oysters, you can watch the shrimp and oyster boats pull into and out of the dock. Add a colorful sunset and you might think you've died and gone to seafood-lovers' heaven.

The building in which Boss Oyster is located was a cotton warehouse and machine shop until the turn of the twentieth century, when the area's fishing industry began to take off. Today, Franklin County, of which Apalachicola is a part, produces 90 percent of Florida's oysters and 10 percent of the country's.

Boss Oyster serves all kinds of seafood—crab, shrimp, scallops, grouper, you name it—but the big attraction is the oysters. Presented on a bed of cracked ice, the enormous raw shellfish sell for $7.75 a dozen, though it's the rare oyster lover who stops at twelve.

On our trip there, we got a bonus. Not only were the oysters wonderful, but we found three small pearls hiding in the shells. They weren't entirely lucky, however. Our waitress still insisted we pay the bill.

Boss Oyster is located in the Apalachicola River Inn at 125 Water Street. Phone (850) 653-9364 or log on to www.apalachicolariverinn.com.

TALK FAST, CHIEF, I'M RUNNING OUT OF QUARTERS
Carrabelle

The middle of the Panhandle on the Gulf of Mexico is called the Forgotten Coast because it resembles (for now) what Florida looked like before Yankee transplants and condominiums ruined everything.

In the heart of the Forgotten Coast is Carrabelle, where somebody forgot to build a proper police station. The blue phone booth at the corner of US 98 and County Road 67 has been described as the World's Smallest Police Station. What many people don't realize is that when the phone booth was erected in 1963, it was an improvement over the old police communications facility, a phone on the wall across the street.

"Every time it rained, the man who answered the phone would get wet," said former Police Chief Jesse Smith.

When he was not patrolling, Smith parked by the phone booth. "We'd just sit there because there was a little shade and it's right in the middle of town. We could see everything that was going on, and if people needed to get ahold of us, they'd call and we'd answer the phone." (You could ring up the police station/phone booth then by dialing 3691. Phone number prefixes were apparently another forgotten thing in Carrabelle.)

*The world's smallest police station, in Carrabelle, is about
the size of a phone booth and is occasionally stolen by
college students.*

In 1991, Smith told Johnny Carson all about the World's
Smallest Police Station on the *Tonight Show,* and the little cop
shop was also featured on *Real People.* Today, visitors from
around the world visit Carrabelle to have their picture taken
next to the police booth, which was replaced years ago by a
more conventional police station that late-night comedians have
thus far ignored. In fact, there's no longer even a phone in the
booth, thanks in part to tourists making unauthorized long-
distance calls and college students trying to steal the whole
package. (They were caught, and the phone booth was returned
to its rightful place. Just because they work out of a phone
booth doesn't mean Carrabelle police aren't alert.)

Today, you might find a Carrabelle patrol car parked in the vicinity of the tiny old police station, but visitors who want more information about the history of the thing would be better off popping into Carrabelle Realty next door, where transplanted Brit Rene Topping is glad to answer questions and offer up anecdotes, including the one about the 300-pound deputy who was too fat to squeeze inside the phone booth.

From her we learned that Carrabelle, a working man's village of 1,400 souls devoted mostly to commercial fishing, once played an important role in World War II by serving as a huge military training facility. More than 30,000 troops were stationed here and on nearby Dog Island in an assemblage of 1,100 buildings called Camp Gordon Johnston. There was a bombing range, a bazooka range, a bayonet and knife course, and what would surely be our least favorite obstacle, a series of shell holes and trenches where machine guns would fire live ammunition just 30 inches above the ground while troops crawled underneath.

Hello? Carrabelle police? Is anyone there? HELP!!!

W O R M   F I D D L I N '
C a r y v i l l e

If you fiddle, they will come.

The "they" in this case is worms. Big fat night crawlers. Lots of 'em.

JoAn Palmer of the Panhandle town of Caryville is the best worm fiddler in these parts and quite possibly in the whole state. She and a friend once fiddled up 205 worms in five minutes in a 6-by-6-foot square of ground. That's a lot of fish bait.

Mrs. Palmer explains the art of worm fiddlin' this way:

"You take a sharpened two-by-four and hammer it into the ground with the back of an ax. Then you run the blade of the ax up and down the board so it makes an eh-eh-eh sound."

The eh-eh-eh sound does not translate well in the printed word, but apparently to worms' ears, assuming worms have ears, it sounds like the music in the shower scene of *Psycho*.

"One boy stuck a truck spring in the ground and ran his ax over it," Mrs. Palmer continued. "It's the vibration that brings the worms up."

Worm fiddling, sometimes it's called snoring worms, is practiced throughout the South, but Caryville might be the only place that chose to make it the centerpiece of an annual festival. Most every Labor Day going back to 1976 (floods and droughts have canceled the festival on several occasions) people would come from miles around to watch Mrs. Palmer, her husband, Jack, and anyone else with an ax to grind fiddle up some worms. There was always music and plenty of food. (No worm burgers, however.)

The festival took a nosedive after the big flood of 1994 when the Choctawhatchee River overflowed its banks and inundated the tiny town. The Palmers, who had 4 feet of water in their living room, were one of the few families who chose to stay, rebuilding their house on higher ground. The last Worm Fiddling Festival was in 1996, but Mrs. Palmer isn't ruling out a comeback.

"If enough people show an interest, we'll do it again, I guess," she said.

Until such time, her fiddlin' record of 205 worms in five minutes should be safe.

Caryville is located off Interstate 10 about 8 miles west of Bonifay.

BREAKING OFF THE PANHANDLE

The Panhandle region of Florida, extending west nearly to Mobile, Alabama, is more Southern than south Florida. There are more young natives and fewer northern retirees. More grits and fewer bagels. The drawls can be as thick as those grits, and the Civil War is still sometimes referred to as simply "the wah."

The Florida capital is part of the Panhandle, but state representatives from Miami are closer to Havana than they are to Tallahassee.

If the southeastern United States made geographical sense, Florida's capital would be near Orlando, and the Panhandle would be part of Alabama. What's almost forgotten in state history is that this division almost happened after the Civil War. Florida offered to sell the territory to Alabama. The war-depleted Cotton State couldn't come up with the money, so the Panhandle coastline, now known as "The Redneck Riviera," remained a part of Florida.

THE KUDZU ALSO RISES
Chipley

You see it everywhere in the South, climbing trees and utility poles, wrapping itself around sheds and abandoned cars, blanketing the landscape like a lush green quilt.

Kudzu is the polite name for it. Less flattering names include cuss you, the foot-a-night vine, and the vine that ate the South. That last characterization is not far wrong: Kudzu covers seven million acres in the Deep South and would surely cover more if people weren't working so hard to get rid of the fast-growing weed.

Kudzu did not always have a bad reputation. You could say it grew into it. The oriental vine was first introduced to this country in 1876 when the Japanese used it to shade their exhibit booth at the U.S. Centennial Exposition in Philadelphia. The idea caught on, and people from Virginia to Alabama began planting the stuff as a porch vine.

Enter Charles E. and Lillie Pleas, a kindly Quaker couple who had relocated from Indiana to tiny Chipley in northwest Florida. Both naturalists, the Pleas discovered that animals would eat the plant, so they began promoting its use as forage in the 1920s. Their Glen Arden Nursery sold kudzu plants through the mail. A historical marker on the site of the old nursery, now the Washington County Agricultural Center on US 90, proudly proclaims KUDZU DEVELOPED HERE.

During the Great Depression of the 1930s, the Soil Conservation Service promoted kudzu for erosion control. (Its very ability to hold soil in place is what makes it so hard to kill; kudzu's roots can extend 8 feet into the earth.) Hundreds of young men were given work planting kudzu through the Civilian Conservation Corps. Farmers were paid as much as eight dollars an acre as incentive to plant fields of the vines in the 1940s.

The problem with kudzu is that it grows too well, smothering native crops and plants and covering trees so densely that they die for lack of light. The vine can grow as quickly as a foot a day, and some herbicides actually make it grow faster. After the USDA declared kudzu a weed in 1972, it's all been pretty much downhill for the vine ever since.

While there are many who wish the Pleas had been a little less successful in promoting kudzu, the plant is not universally hated. Basket makers do great things with the rubberlike vines, a South Carolina woman makes paper from kudzu, and you can find kudzu blossom jelly, kudzu syrup, kudzu burgers, even kudzu wine. (We'll just have a Coke, thank you.)

There are several kudzu festivals around the southeast, but none, sadly, in Chipley, the adopted home of kudzu pioneers Charles and Lillie Pleas.

"I guess a lot of people around here would just as soon keep quiet about that," said Chipley Mayor Tommy McDonald.

The marker commemorating the Pleases' achievement (abomination) is located in front of the Washington County Agricultural Center on US 90 in downtown Chipley. The Pleas are buried in the Glenwood Cemetery on Glenwood Avenue. Their side-by-side graves, about two-thirds the way back, on the right, are marked by a tombstone that reads KUDZU PIONEERS. If you have trouble locating it, ring up Mayor Tommy McDonald at City Hall (850–638–6350) and ask him if he'd be so kind as to drive you out.

WHO YOU CALLIN' A REDNECK?
Chumuckla

The Chumuckla Redneck Parade got its start nine years ago when some good old boys got into the Jack Daniels on Christmas Eve and had to be led home by their wives. Some parade, somewhere, has probably been inspired by less, but we can't think of one offhand.

"It started as a joke," said parade coordinator Kathy Barr, "but it caught on and kept growing."

Today, nearly 10,000 people come from as far away as Dothan, Alabama, and Fort Walton Beach to watch or participate in the Redneck Parade, which is held every year on the second Sunday in December.

"It's always the weekend after the Snowball Derby [a local stock-car race]," said Barr. "We would never want to interfere with that."

It's easy to participate in the Redneck Parade. All you need to do is make a $1.00 donation and contribute a food item. The money is used to buy stuff for the local community center and kids' activities; the food is given to needy families. Before you sign up, it would probably be a good idea to go out and buy yourself a set of Bubba Teeth. Bubba Teeth, for those of you who are unfamiliar with the things (that would include us, until Kathy Barr filled us in), are splayed, discolored fake choppers with more than a few gaps. Think of the dental work of the hillbillies in *Deliverance* and you've got a pretty good picture. Bubba Teeth are, needless to say, available in all of the finer convenience stores in and around Chumuckla.

Feel free to create your own redneck-themed float. A popular one in the 2001 parade was Santa Claus in a bathtub pulled by a go-cart. (No, we weren't aware Santa Claus was a redneck either. The Redneck Parade is nothing if not instructive.)

And no Florida celebration, festival, or parade would be complete without some sort of beauty pageant, or in this case, lack-of-beauty pageant. The 2001 King and Queen Redneck were Charles Barr and Angie Kilpatrick. Charles, Kathy's husband (conflict of interest?), is six-four, weighs 375 pounds, and sports a bushy beard. In his pageant getup of shorts, tennis shoes, and ball cap, Kathy said he resembled an "oversized Viking."

Angie Kilpatrick chose for her costume a prom dress (naturally), about forty pounds of makeup, a hairdo comprising three different kinds of pigtails, and, of course, Bubba Teeth.

Everyone agreed that they made a lovely couple.

Chumuckla is located about 25 miles northeast of Pensacola on County Road 182. Don't blink or you'll miss it; there's not even so much as a traffic light. For more information on the Redneck Parade, call Kathy Barr at (850) 994–5505.

WHEN LOVE IS IN THE AIR
Marianna

If you drive through Florida in May or September, you might notice—no, you definitely *will* notice—that the air is thick with some sort of slow-moving black fly. Then you will notice that the flies make no effort to get out of the way, and your windshield (not to mention your headlights, grille, and radiator) is soon covered by a thick layer of sticky gore.

This is how most people are first introduced to love bugs, so named because the male and the female of the species fly around in love's embrace, hoping to end their lives Romeo-and-

Juliet style on the windshield of a passing Oldsmobile.

The bane of motorists and the boon of car washes, love bugs do not sting or bite or carry any diseases. They just make love (preferably over highways; they're attracted by auto exhaust) until the smaller male drops off dead or the tandem splats against a windshield, whichever comes first. They lead a rather one-dimensional life, love bugs.

Your average Floridian is a lot more familiar with love bugs than he is with swamp cabbage or manatees or conchs, so it was just a matter of time before somebody came up with the idea of a Love Bug Festival.

That man is Ted Eubanks, and his celebration of the bug of love takes place the first weekend in June at the fairgrounds in Marianna. There is the usual assortment of arts and crafts, food vendors, sack races, and pony rides, but the highlight of the festival is the crowning of Little Miss Love Bug.

We asked Ted if Little Miss Love Bug celebrates her victory by killing Little Mister Love Bug or by pasting herself on the windshield of a passing VW Beetle. Happily (or sadly, depending on how sick you are), Miss Love Bug does neither. She simply thanks the judges and then moseys off for a funnel cake and maybe some ribs.

Ted says he hopes to add more love-buggy elements to future festivals, including a costume parade.

"About all we have now is a 2-inch-by-2-inch love bug house," he says. "Love bugs could fly in there if they wanted to, but so far they haven't."

Marianna is located about 60 miles northwest of Tallahassee off US 90. For more information, call (850) 526–7777.

AGAINST ALL ODDS

The Seminole is the only tribe of American Indians that never signed a peace treaty with the United States.

Fat lot of good it did them.

Calling themselves the "Unconquered People," the Florida tribe was reduced to fewer than 300 people after three wars with the United States between 1817 and 1858. At one point, 3,000 poorly armed warriors were pitted against four U.S. generals and more than 200,000 troops. This, the Second Seminole War (1835–1842), was the fiercest and most expensive war ever waged by the U.S. government against Native Americans. The low point came in 1837 when Gen. Thomas Jesup, flying a truce flag, lured the great Seminole leader Osceola into a trap. Captured, Osceola was shipped off to prison at Fort Moultrie, near Charleston, South Carolina, where he died a year later.

By 1858, after years of war, more than 3,000 Seminoles had been uprooted and relocated west of the Mississippi, mostly in Oklahoma. One of them was Billy Bowlegs, the Seminole leader in the Third Seminole War (1855-1858). Bowlegs and his war-weary band surrendered on May 7, 1858, after the U.S. government promised him a substantial amount of money for his land. Thirty-eight warriors and eighty-five women and children, including Billy's wife, boarded the steamer Grey Cloud *at Egmont Key, south of Tampa, to begin their journey to Indian territory in what is now Oklahoma. Billy was never compensated, and he died on April 27, 1859, after a brief stint in the Union Army.*

Things didn't begin to turn around for the Seminoles until 1970, when the Indian Claims Commission awarded the Seminoles (of both Oklahoma and Florida) $12,347,500 for the land taken from them by the U.S. military. The Seminole tribe was recognized as an entity separate from the state of Florida and the United States. In 1977, the Seminoles opened the first tax-free "smoke shop," selling discount cigarettes and tobacco products. The opening of the tribe's first high-stakes bingo hall in Hollywood was a national first, and gaming has since become the largest single source of revenue for Native Americans.

Today, more than 2,000 descendants of the last 300 Florida Seminoles live on six reservations in the state: Hollywood, Big Cypress, Brighton, Immokalee, Fort Pierce, and Tampa.

The Seminole canoe has been replaced by cars, airplanes, and airboats, and instead of telling stories around the fire, Seminoles, like most modern Americans, prefer to watch TV.

The county of Osceola, near Disney World in east central Florida, was named after the Indian leader. Micanopy (pronounced mick-a-NO-pee), a town in Alachua County popular with antique hunters, is named after the Seminole leader of the Second Seminole War. His name translates to "top chief." Okeechobee, the huge lake in south central Florida, comes from the Seminole for "big water."

There are at least five Florida sports teams called the Seminoles, not the least of which is the FSU Seminoles, based at Florida State University in Tallahassee. Many other Florida town and place-names have Seminole roots.

ITCHING TO HAVE A PARTY
Milton

Back in the good old days, before the invention of insect repellent or a decent pair of wading boots, the pioneers who founded the Panhandle town of Milton had to slog through the marshes and swamps of the Blackwater River. The mucky trek resulted in numerous mosquito bites, not to mention briar and sandspur scratches to the ankle and leg. It must have been bad, because the pioneers began calling themselves Scratch Ankles, a nickname that residents of Milton continue to use to this day.

Of course nothing is official until you have a celebration in its honor, which explains the Scratch Ankle Festival held every spring in Milton for the past thirty years. There aren't any contests involving barefoot runs through briar patches, but you can gorge on hot dogs and funnel cakes and listen to local bands play country music and gospel. The highlight of the event, which usually takes place in late March, is the coronation of Little Mr. and Miss Scratch Ankle, a pageant open only to couples between the ages of four and six. It is, needless to say, unbearably cute and, we understand, quite competitive.

No word on whether there is a runner-up that can step up to serve the remainder of the term if the winning couple is unable to fulfill their duties, whatever they may be. Learning the alphabet, perhaps.

The Scratch Ankle Festival is held on State Road 87 between Berryhill and Park Avenues. For more information, call (850) 983–5400.

THE "CHIC MAYBERRY" OF
THE PANHANDLE
Seaside

The Panhandle resort town of Seaside, a model home for "New Urbanism" in Florida, served as a backdrop for the 1996 Jim Carrey movie *The Truman Show*. To express a vision of ersatz Americana, producers needed a super-stereotypical small town with brick streets, picket fences, and everything within easy walking distance. Seaside fit the bill.

After filming ended, a few fake storefronts were left standing for a while, because founder Robert Davis liked the way they looked. This says a little something about the genuine unreality of Seaside.

Davis, along with architects Andres Duany and Elizabeth Plater-Zyberk, built Seaside on a gorgeous stretch of Panhandle coastline in 1982. It was a revelation in urban planning, receiving universal acclaim for being pedestrian-friendly, promoting bold colors and metal roofs, and banning lawns in favor of natural landscaping.

What was planned as a modest community, however, quickly became a weekend getaway for the wealthy citizens of Montgomery and Birmingham, New Orleans and Atlanta. And now the quiet coastal highway is jammed with Seaside imitators and anti-Seaside sprawl.

For a twentieth anniversary story, the *Palm Beach Post* called Seaside a "chic Mayberry." Others aren't so kind. Detractors who'd like to hate the place need look no further than the oh-so-cutesy name of a Seaside trinket shop.

Sue Vaneers.

WAY DOWN UPON THE RACIST LYRICS

The Suwannee is a scenic 250-mile river that meanders south from Okeefenokee Swamp in Georgia to the Gulf of Mexico, forming (more or less) the eastern boundary of the Florida Panhandle. However pretty it may be, the Suwannee was just another river until it was made famous by the 1851 hit single, "Swannee River," also known as "Old Folks at Home."

The river's big break almost never happened. Composer Stephen Foster originally chose Pennsylvania's Peedee River as the song's namesake. Foster wisely decided that the lyric "way down upon the Peedee River" might not capture the public's imagination; after consulting an atlas, he settled on the far more mellifluous Suwannee.

The atlas was as close as Foster ever came to the Suwannee, or to Florida for that matter. Born in Pittsburgh in 1826, Foster spent his entire life in the North, where he became the most prolific and successful songwriter of his day. It's too bad they didn't have greatest-hits albums back in those days, because Foster's would have been a monster. Besides "Old Folks at Home," he penned "Beautiful Dreamer," "Camptown Races," "Jeanie with the Light Brown Hair," "Oh! Susanna," "My Old Kentucky Home," and, as they like to say on the late-night commercials, "many, many more."

Foster is to be credited—or blamed—for launching Florida's tourist industry. "Swannee River" sold hundreds of thousands of copies, and, starting in the late 1800s, folks from Up North began coming to Florida, seeking the quaint, happy plantation world that Foster made up for the purposes of his song. The tune had such an impact that the Florida legislature made it the official state song in 1935. Unfortunately, the lyrics of "Swannee River" have become a tad—how shall we say?—dated. To put it another way, it's not the first song we'd choose to sing at our next Kwanzaa party. Here's how the original lyrics begin:

Way down upon de Swannee Ribber,
Far, far away,
Dere's wha my heart is turning ebber,
Dere's wha de old folks stay.
All up and down de whole creation
Sadly I roam,
Still longing for de old plantation,
And for de old folks at home.

All de world am sad and dreary,
Eb-rywhere I roam;
Oh, darkeys, how my heart grows weary,
Far from de old folks at home!

Perhaps to prevent a riot, the word "brothers" was substituted for "darkeys" when the song was sung at the dedication of the new Florida capitol building in 1978. Modern published versions of the song also eliminate the dialect.

Maybe everyone would have been better off if Florida had stuck with its original state song, adopted in 1913 and titled "Florida, My Florida." Written in 1894 by Rev. Dr. C. V. Waugh, a professor of languages at the Florida Agricultural College at Lake City, the song was said by the legislature to have "both metric and patriotic merit of the kind calculated to inspire love for home and native State." Sung to the tune of "Maryland, My Maryland," one verse goes like this:

The golden fruit the world outshines
Florida, my Florida
Thy gardens and thy phosphate mines
Florida, my Florida.

Ah, yes. What Floridian's eyes don't get a little misty thinking about those lovely phosphate mines? "Swannee River" has its faults, granted, but at least it doesn't ask us to get nostalgic over some big ugly holes in the ground.

HOW A PANHANDLE TOWN WAS HATCHED
Two Egg

With the Pittman grocery long closed, and the crumbling old Hart store scheduled to be demolished, the Lawrence Grocery Store remains the heart and soul of Two Egg, Florida, a crossroads town northeast of Marianna. The sagging wood-frame building provides a single Chevron gas pump and sells candy bars and plumbing fixtures, cigarettes and car batteries, *Florida Farmer* magazine and the *Jackson County News*. Nell King, the native who bought the store thirteen years ago, knows everyone in town, which isn't that hard, considering the local population.

"It's probably about thirty-two; that's what it says on the sign," she says. "We have to count 'em up if someone dies or moves out."

King lives next door to the grocery store in a small house behind a big oak tree. The license plate on her car reads TWO EGG 1. Her husband, of course, is TWO EGG 2. Back at the store, some of the most popular items for sale are Two Egg souvenirs.

There are Two Egg caps, T-shirts, and sweatshirts. Two Egg greeting cards and Two Egg license plates. Two Egg paintings by Marian Oswald of nearby Bascom, Florida. Finally, there's Two Egg cane syrup made by Robert E. Long, another native of the town—"a Two Eggian," says King, who is used to customers asking questions.

"We have visitors from everywhere, reporters from everywhere," she told us. "Our sign's the most replaced sign in Florida." People steal it all the time.

The folksy name of Two Egg, of course, continues to draw curious tourists and tour groups. There are several versions of the story about how the town was named. Most involve a farm boy trading eggs for candy.

Dick Hinson, an amateur historian of Jackson County, offers to cut through the confusion. "About a hundred years ago, let's say 1910, a traveling salesman—we used to call 'em drummers—was calling on the general store," Hinson says. "A little boy came in with two eggs, and was given a choice of candy from the counter. When the store owner said he was going to name the town, the drummer said he ought to call it Two Egg."

ME TARZAN, YOU JANE
Wakulla Springs

We will resist the temptation to call the waters of Wakulla Springs "gin clear," as it has been our experience that the stuff makes things less clear rather than more. Suffice it to say that the water here is really, really clear. If the light is right, you can see things on the bottom, 185 feet down. In 1850, a woman reportedly spotted the bones of a mastodon at the bottom of the springs. No word on whether gin was involved.

Located about 30 miles south of Tallahassee, Wakulla Springs is the focal point of the Edward Ball Wakulla Springs State Park and Lodge. One of the largest and deepest freshwater springs in the world, Wakulla Springs is fed by an underground river that gushes water at the rate of 400,000 gallons a minute. Divers entering the mouth of the underwater cavern often have their face masks blown off by the force of the current. (Spring Creek Spring, also in Wakulla County, is the state's biggest gusher, emitting 1.3 *billion* gallons of sparkling clear water a day. Take that, Perrier.)

Florida has about 200 freshwater springs, all of them beautiful, but there are several things that make Wakulla unique. For

starters, no one has ever discovered the source of the spring. In
1989, a professional cave diving expedition into the springs
was filmed for a *National Geographic* television special. Other
professional dive teams have traveled more than a mile and
descended more than 300 feet into the honeycomb of limestone
caves beneath the springs. At that point, the cavern branches
into four channels, each tunneling still deeper into the earth.
That's as far as anyone's gotten.

Wakulla Springs is also a popular hangout for slimy man-
like creatures with gills and webbed feet. The movie *The Creature from the Black Lagoon* was filmed here, as were several
early Tarzan movies starring Johnny Weissmuller (the only
real Tarzan, as far as we're concerned), *Airport '77,* and the
unforgettable *Joe Panther.*

The last thing that makes Wakulla Springs unique is the
lodge. The twenty-seven-room retreat was built in 1937 by
Edward Ball, entrepreneur, financier, railroad magnate, and
owner of a big chunk of property surrounding the springs.
Listed on the National Register of Historic Places, the lodge is
a symphony of hand-wrought iron, marble, and imported handmade ceramic tile. But that's not the unique part. The unique
part is that there are no televisions in the rooms! That's right,
folks. If you visit the Wakulla Lodge, you're going to have to
go a whole night without *Supermarket Sweep, Survivor,* or
WWF Smackdown! Consider this before making reservations.

Otherwise, Wakulla is just your typical, otherworldly-
gorgeous Florida spring. The 75 degree waters are a bit of a
shock, even on the hottest summer day. There's a 15-foot-high
diving platform if you want to get it over with right away, or
you can do it like we do and inch in a bit at a time, flapping
your arms and yelling, "OhmigodIt'sCold!" Once in, you'll be
swimming over, around, and with many species of freshwater
fish, including bass, catfish, and bream. And don't be surprised
if you see the occasional alligator. Hey, it's Florida.

Wakulla Springs is located off State Road 363 about 30 miles south of Tallahassee. There is a small admission charge to enter the park. Glass-bottom boat tours are available for an additional fee. For more information or to make reservations, contact Edward Ball Wakulla Springs State Park, 550 Wakulla Park Drive, Wakulla Springs 32305; phone (850) 224–5950. Visit online at www.dep.state.fl.us/park/district1/ wakullasprings/index.asp.

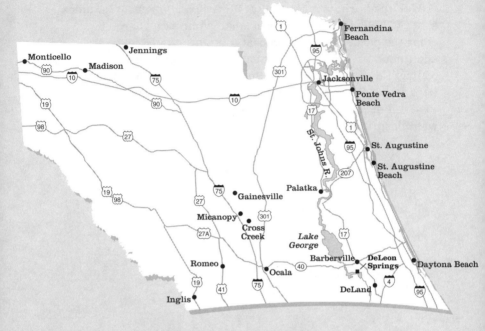

NORTH FLORIDA

NORTH FLORIDA

GIVE US YOUR TIRED, YOUR HUNGRY, YOUR HUDDLED CAROUSEL HORSES YEARNING TO BREATHE FREE
Barberville

If you're in the market for a cast aluminum Statue of Liberty—and who isn't these days?—the place to go is Barberville Produce at the corner of State Road 17 and State Road 40 in, needless to say, Barberville. It may be the only place in America where you can buy a suit of armor and a bag of boiled peanuts at the same time.

Barberville Produce is about all there is to Barberville. At the very least, it's the town's most conspicuous aspect. To say you can't miss it is an understatement. The owner, David Biggers, claims to have a million items strewn about the roadside property. That might be an exaggeration, but not by much. There is stuff of every description and in quantities too numerous to count. Besides the aforementioned Statues of Liberty ($800), there are carousel horses, streetlights, fountains, giant clocks, skulls of longhorn cattle, dancing gators, and innumerable ceramic frogs.

"We have a little bit of this and a little bit of that," says Biggers modestly.

Biggers doesn't make the stuff himself ("That's the first question everyone asks me."); he just sells it. If it doesn't sell, it doesn't stay.

*If you're shopping for a Statue of Liberty—or seven—to embellish
your front lawn, Barberville Produce is the place to go.*

"I don't deal in dead horses," he says.

If true, that's about the only thing he doesn't deal in.

Biggers doesn't put price tags on his merchandise because,
as he likes to say, "this is not Wal-Mart."

Few people would confuse the two. With its cardboard-
covered walkways and jumbled merchandise, Barberville
Produce is more like a flea market, only with weirder stuff.

Though it's rather hard to believe by the looks of the place,
Biggers says he sells mostly to "upscale" customers looking to
enhance the looks of their property with a giant, three-tiered,

cast aluminum fountain or a carousel horse. Restaurants and other businesses "trying to attract attention" buy the Statues of Liberty and suits of armor, and municipalities buy the ornate street lamps to spruce up their business districts.

If you're not in the market for a cattle skull or giant clock, you can buy some fresh fruits and vegetables at the adjoining produce stand.

We highly recommend the boiled peanuts.

Barberville Produce is located at 141 West Highway 40. Hours are 8:00 A.M. to 8:00 P.M., and they are open seven days a week. Phone (386) 749–3562.

THAT'S MR. BOOGER TO YOU
Bardin

L et other states brag about their Bigfoot, Sasquatch, or Abominable Snowman. In northeast Florida, the only mythical hairy monster worth talking about is the Bardin Booger.

Bardin is an almost nonexistent town northwest of Palatka. There used to be a sign on County Road 209A informing motorists that they were entering Bardin, but a car knocked it over a couple of years ago and nobody bothered to put up a new one. The hub, if it can be called that, of Bardin is Bud's Grocery, which used to be the focal point of all things Booger. Old-timers would sit on the front porch of Bud's and discuss the comings and goings of the Booger as casually as people in other towns might talk about the weather. One old boy claimed he saw the Booger running through the woods, carrying a lantern. Another said he saw him snatching laundry off a clothesline. Still another swore he surprised the Booger while the creature was peering in the refrigerator, looking for a snack.

A Florida Curiosities exclusive! A never-before published, unretouched photograph of the reclusive Bardin Booger. Look hard and you can see Elvis at the far end of the tracks.

The Booger has made itself scarce for about the past forty years, leading some to speculate that it either died or moved to a place less populated, like maybe Mars. (Actually, the new home of the Booger is believed to be Welatka, an even less wide place in the road south of Bardin.)

Today, all that is left of the legend is Lena Crain, a perky, diminutive Palatka woman who tends the Booger's flame—or lantern, as it were—by dressing up in a modified gorilla suit and entertaining guests at the local Moose Club.

It is a calling she takes very seriously. Her late husband, Billy, wrote a ballad about the Bardin Booger called, appropriately enough, "The Bardin Booger." Lena followed up with her own composition, "The Bardin Booger's Christmas Wish," which is musically significant in two ways: (1) we learn the Booger wants a wife for Christmas, and (2) it is the only known recording that attempts to rhyme the words "brief" and "wish."

"I think there's something out there," said Lena Crain. "I'm just not sure what. A circus came to this area some years back. Maybe a gorilla escaped and mated with something."

Lena's Booger costume is a reflection of that suspicion. It's basically a gorilla suit onto which she sewed a pair of ears. She also painted the lips red and the teeth white, just to jazz it up a bit. She takes her act to service club meetings, schools, festivals, wherever the services of a Booger are needed. Unlike her woodsy counterpart, Lena is a gentle, people-friendly kind of Booger who takes great pains not to frighten the children.

"The little ones get scared if you growl or jump around too much," she explains.

Her act is usually accompanied by Billy's song, the chorus of which goes like this:

Hey, Mr. Bardin Booger!
Bardin is your home.
And every day you love to roam.
You run through the bushes and you run through the trees.
Hey, Mr. Bardin Booger,
Don't you get me, please!

Besides inspiring a couple of songs, the prospect of an odiferous half-gorilla, half-something roaming the piney woods of northeast Florida proved to be a crude but effective disciplinary tool.

"Parents had no trouble keeping their kids close to home," Lena said. "They told them if they strayed too far, the Booger would get them."

Meanwhile, back at Bud's Grocery, which, by the way, carries stovepipes if you happen to need one, we asked clerk Norma Key if she had any personal knowledge of the Bardin Booger.

"I sure do," she said. "I married him."

MARJORIE KINNAN RAWLINGS AND THE YEARLING
Cross Creek

A tour of the Marjorie Kinnan Rawlings Historic State Park begins with a marker and excerpt from *Cross Creek,* her 1942 novel: "It is necessary to leave the impersonal highway, to step inside the rusty gate and leave it behind. One is now inside the orange grove, out of one world and in the mysterious heart of another. And after long years of spiritual homelessness, of nostalgia, here is that mystic loveliness of childhood again. Here is home."

The fact that this placard stands in an orange grove, just inside a rusty gate, is letter perfect.

For literary fans of *Cross Creek* and *The Yearling,* the latter made into a movie with Gregory Peck, the Rawlings site covers familiar ground. She wrote about her farm house, citrus groves, and nearby Orange Lake, and here they all are. On the broad screened veranda where Rawlings served meals, an orange tabby cat surveys visitors with sleepy eyes.

Rawlings moved to the seventy-two-acre farm in 1928, after a spring vacation in Florida. She began writing and won the Pulitzer Prize in 1938 for *The Yearling*, the story of a young boy and his fawn coming of age.

She later wrote *Cross Creek* and then *Cross Creek Cookery*, as someone confident of her culinary capabilities. "For my part, my literary ability may safely be questioned as harshly as one wills," Rawlings wrote, "but indifference to my table puts me into a rage."

The Marjorie Kinnan Rawlings Historic State Park is southeast of Gainesville on County Road 325 in Cross Creek. Admission is $3.00 for adults, $2.00 for children. For more information, call (352) 466–3672.

CHANGING FLATS FOR FUN?
Daytona Beach

After a long drive to Florida, most tourists have had enough of roads and traffic, lines and delays, noise and fumes. Car sickness, to one degree or another, is common. The very idea of having to change a flat tire, in a hurry and with crowds watching, is enough to send them over the edge.

At Daytona USA, people pay for the privilege.

The motorsports attraction offers NASCAR exhibits, motion simulators, and tours of the world-famous Daytona International Speedway. Then there's the Ford 16-Second Pit Stop Challenge, in which visitors race to change a race car tire. Never have so many people enjoyed handling a car jack, power drill, and oversize tire.

As of yet, Daytona USA doesn't have any blown radiator challenges or fiery collision simulators.

What it does have are museum displays that trace the history of racing on Daytona Beach, where the firm-packed sand first drew cars in the early 1900s. Later on, Bill France, the founder of NASCAR, designed a beach race course and charged admission. To discourage gate-crashers, he posted signs that read BEWARE OF RATTLESNAKES.

Now that NASCAR has become such a huge success, filling 150,000-seat stadiums, attendance is not a problem. Daytona USA puts the bite on enthusiastic fans by charging extra for the Dream Laps and Acceleration Alley simulator games. The Pit Stop Challenge, though, is still included in the general admission price.

Apparently, charging people extra to change tires would be asking too much.

Daytona USA is at 1801 West International Speedway Boulevard, Daytona Beach. Admission is $20.00 for adults, $13.00 for seniors, $8.00 for children six to twelve. Children under six get in free. Hours are 9:00 A.M. to 7:00 P.M. every day except Christmas, with extended hours during peak times. For more information, call (386) 947–6782.

F LORIDA'S W ORLD-FAMOUS B IKE W EEK
Daytona Beach

Each year, thousands of motorcyclists roar into Daytona Beach for Bike Week, a celebration that is half reunion, half trade show, and half Mardi Gras. If this adds up to more than a whole, well, that's the general idea. The annual motorcycle extravaganza offers races and rallies, parties and concerts, smoke shops and strip shows, but everything begins with the daily parade of bikes down Main Street, where the traffic signs read MOTORCYCLES ONLY.

If you haven't cruised the strip, then you haven't been to Bike Week.

*Even the dogs like to look sharp during Bike Week in
Daytona Beach, as Spike the beagle demonstrates.*

When a Harley-Davidson kicks to a start, with an open throt-
tle and fat pipes, you can feel it in your boots. When one hundred Harleys rumble from a curb, and the leather chaps crowd
cheers at the corner of Main Street and Atlantic Avenue, you
can feel it in your bones. This is the sight, sound, and over-
whelming sensation of Bike Week.

"The big event is this, Main Street," said Rich Hand, a New
York City rider making his tenth trip to Daytona Beach in
2002. "Just people walking by, looking over the bikes, having a
good time."

There are lots of bikers at Bike Week. More bikers than
you've ever seen before. More than you'll ever see anywhere
else. Fat bikers and skinny bikers. Old bikers and young bik-
ers. Bald bikers, bikers with hair, and bikers with ponytails.
Bikers on laid-back choppers, and bikers on forward-leaning
racers. Bikers with babes, bikers with kids, bikers with kids in
sidecars.

There are bikers who look like Neil Young. Bikers who look
like Vince Neil. Bikers who look like Neil Sedaka.

WELCOME BIKERS. TRIKE WORLD AND BIKERS DEPOT. JIM BEAM—
AIN'T A BIKER BAR WITHOUT IT. AMERICAN KNIGHTS OF CHICAGO.
PLEASE RIDE QUIET.

There seems to be lots of drinking on Daytona Beach, and
some ladies flashing and men hollering, but old-timers agree
that Bike Week ain't so bad these days. Tourism might be the
great equalizer. Even the burliest biker doesn't look so tough
toting a bright shopping bag from Yukon Jack's Custom
Leather. Even the toughest tough guy looks a little silly taking
out a disposable camera for a souvenir snapshot. Lots of bikers
bring their families these days, and some bike-watchers roll
babies in strollers.

On one crowded corner of Main Street, surrounded by griz-
zled guys in Harley black, two young flutists played quietly for
tips. A sign explained that the local girls were raising money
for a band trip to France. A block down the street, Ed Zima of
South Daytona Beach posed for photos with his dog Spike, a
beagle.

"Every year they get pictures of Spike," Zima said proudly.
"He's four years old; I've been coming since '77." What makes
Ed and Spike such an attraction? Well, both the dog and owner
wear matching leather vests and caps.

Bike Week is held in late February or early March each year.
For more information, phone (386) 255–0981 or log on to
www.daytonachamber.com.

THE SKYDIVING GURU OF DELAND
DeLand

If skydiving has a world capital, it's DeLand, Florida, a small university town north of Orlando. SkyDive DeLand is a leading drop zone, and *Skydiving* magazine is published just a few blocks from the municipal airport. There are two harness makers nearby, along with the world's largest maker of parachute canopies. There's also Bill Booth, the free thinker who patented modern chute rigging and revolutionized the sport with tandem skydiving.

Booth, 55, is a Miami native who wears a ZZ Top beard and lives in a pyramid-shaped house on a lake just outside of town. Although he graduated from the University of Florida with a degree in music education, of all things, he also had an engineering background, along with a passion for skydiving and perfect timing.

"When I started jumping in 1965, the gear was basically unchanged from 1918, so I came along at the right time," he says. "I'm not an engineer type; I'm an inventor type. I think differently than other people, apparently."

Booth taught skydiving before developing the rigging that is found on virtually all modern parachutes. He also helped come up with the idea of tandem rigging that would allow an instructor to accompany a student to the ground. There was only one way to test the idea.

"I took my secretary and just went up and did it," he says.

After delicate negotiations with the Federal Aeronautics Administration (he'd broken regulations by making these development flights) he got approval for tandem skydiving. It's

Bill Booth revolutionized skydiving and help put DeLand on the map—he's also the hands-down winner of the ZZ Top look-alike contest.

revolutionized the sport, giving beginners a chance for the full skydiving experience. Along the way, Booth became something of a celebrity.

"When I made *National Geographic,* my mom was impressed," he boasts. "When I made MTV, my kids were impressed."

Tom Cruise took skydiving lessons while filming *Days of Thunder* in nearby Daytona Beach. He got to know Booth, and later got him a bit part in *The Firm.* One of Booth's favorite stories is about another skydiving student asking him to sign his log book after a training jump.

"This kid comes up with a pen, walks right past Tom Cruise, and says, 'Are you Bill Booth?'" he says, laughing. "And Cruise's jaw just dropped. I said, 'I bet that never happened to you before.' So for once in my life I upstaged Tom Cruise."

Today Booth continues to run his company, Relative Workshop, which he's renamed The Uninsured Relative Workshop to help reduce liability. He's known throughout the skydiving world for both tandem jumps and his trademark beard. That personal touch dates back to his days as a close-cropped schoolteacher.

"I always said if I had my own company, I'd never shave again," he says. "Now I'm like Colonel Sanders, and I'm stinking stuck with it."

THE FLIP-YOUR-OWN-PANCAKE RESTAURANT
DeLeon Springs

Seven miles north of DeLand, within the DeLeon Springs State Recreation Area, is the Old Spanish Sugar Mill Grill and Griddle House. Moss-draped oaks line the road to the restaurant, and the front door is just a few feet from the crystal-clear water of the natural spring. The Sugar Mill Grill starts serving breakfast at 9:00 A.M. on weekdays, 8:00 A.M. on the weekends, and lots of people will wait an hour or two in line for a table.

The secret to this success? There's an electric griddle in the center of each table where you cook your own pancakes, eggs, and French toast. Waitresses bring out all the ingredients, including flour ground on French buhrstones, and the whole thing is homey and fun. Patricia Schwarze, who took over the place from her father, doesn't know of any other restaurant like it.

"It's a lot of work, an astounding amount of work, considering that people cook their own food," she says, laughing. "But you need extra staff and, from a restaurant point of view, the tables turn over really slowly. It's insane, quite frankly, but we have a lot of fun with it. It's the play interaction that makes it work. We give people batter and let them play."

Patricia's father, a fifth-generation gristmiller, had a New York bakery in the 1920s. He'd set a griddle on the counter, and it would become a convivial meeting place for local customers. Years later, Schwarze brought the idea to Florida, after restoring the old mill at DeLeon Springs in 1961.

"He was a character, quite the raconteur," Patricia says. "Those are my early memories, of sitting around here with the storytellers."

The Sugar Mill Grill remains a distinctive place. A huge mill wheel dominates one side of the restaurant, and there's a brick fireplace along another wall. Payment is on something like an honor system. On the way out, you tell the cashier what you had, and she rings it up on the cash register.

If cooking customers get a little too boisterous or messy, there's a waitress who jokes that they'll be washing their dishes too.

DeLeon Springs State Recreation Area is 7 miles north of DeLand on State Road 17. The Old Spanish Sugar Mill Grill and Griddle House is open from 9:00 A.M. to 4:00 P.M. on weekdays, 8:00 A.M. to 4:00 P.M. on weekends. Pancakes are $4.00 per person. Expect a long wait in line in winter and on weekends. For more information, call (386) 985–4212.

EIGHT FLAGS OVER AMELIA ISLAND
Fernandina Beach

You've heard of Six Flags over Texas? Forget that. Florida's Amelia Island, north of Jacksonville, has a checkered history that requires unflagging attention. No fewer than eight banners have flown over the island.

First there were the French. Jean Ribault named the place Isle de Mai after landing on May 3, 1562. Next came the Spanish, who defeated the French and founded St. Augustine down the coast. They named the island Santa Maria after a mission there.

That mission was destroyed in 1702 by the English, who named the island Amelia in honor of the daughter of George II. Following the Revolutionary War, Britain ceded Florida back to Spain. Thomas Jefferson's Embargo Act closed U.S. ports to shipping, and Fernandina Beach became infamous for smugglers and pirates.

With U.S. backing, the "Patriots of Amelia Island" overthrew the Spanish in 1812 and raised their own flag, replacing it with the Stars and Stripes the next day. Spain demanded the island back and built Fort San Carlos, only to see it seized by Sir Gregor MacGregor, who raised the Green Cross of Florida flag over the fort in 1817. He withdrew, but later that year another uprising brought the Mexican Rebel flag to the island.

Finally, in 1821, Spain ceded Amelia Island to the United States, which built Fort Clinch on the north shore. Confederate forces took the fort briefly during the Civil War, but Union troops regained the island in 1862. It's been part of the United States ever since, through boom and bust, pulp mills and shrimp fleets, and now boasts of luxury resorts such as the Ritz-Carlton and Amelia Island Plantation.

For those keeping score at home, Amelia Island history goes something like this: French, Spanish, English, Spanish, Patriots, Green Cross of Florida, Mexican Rebel, United States, Confederate States, United States.

TRULY NOLEN'S MOUSE MOBILES

*F*lorida residents learn to take them for granted, like sunshine and fresh orange juice, but the bright yellow vehicles draw stares from newcomers and tourists. Once the color catches their eyes, the whimsical mouse ears and tail usually draw a smile or two. How often do you see a mouse mobile rolling down the highway?

The fact that these vehicles advertise a pest control company takes some explaining.

Truly Nolen, the son of a Miami exterminator, graduated from the University of Florida with a degree in entomology. He moved to Tucson, Arizona, in 1955 to start his own bug business. When his wife's car broke down, he painted his name and number on the side as a garage billboard of sorts. People responded, so he bought another car, and then another one. By 1961 Nolen had expanded to Florida, tried painting a truck red to represent a fire ant, and then decided on bright yellow Volkswagen Beetles with black ears, whiskers, and tails.

The rest is pest control advertising history.

Today Truly Nolen is the third largest exterminating company in the country, and mouse mobiles roll across most of Arizona and Florida. The cars are accompanied by silly catchphrases such as "Adios, cucaracha" and "Nite-nite, termite." An employee coined the latest slogan, "Ears and tails above the rest," to win a company contest.

Truly Nolen is an unusual name to begin with, and the mice make it even more memorable.

"It's a great icebreaker," says Barry Murray, director of company public relations in Hollywood, Florida. "Some of our drivers get scared, because people will jump out at a red light and start snapping pictures. Some of our single sales guys say it's a chick magnet too."

The cars have also drawn attention at the other Hollywood, the one in California. In the 2000 Burt Reynolds movie The Crew, hapless bank robbers use a mouse mobile to pull off a heist.

"We've been in about six movies, and we've never paid to be in one," Murray says. "They call us. Everyone knows our humorous edge."

Truly Nolen's mouse mobiles have evolved and improved over the years. The metal ears used to slow the cars down, because they blocked so much wind, so an employee came with the idea of hinges that allow them to lay back at speeds greater than 25 miles per hour. Today the mice are the second most recognized advertising vehicle in the country, after the Oscar Meyer Wienermobile.

Among children, the Truly Nolen vehicles are especially popular.

"We're the only pest control company that gets called for car day at schools, along with the fire trucks and everything," Murray says. "That's always dangerous, though, because we know we'll have a broken tail by the end of the day. So we always bring an extra one."

GLOW-IN-THE-DARK BICYCLES
Gainesville

About thirty-five years ago, Gatorade was developed by researchers at the University of Florida. It began as a greenish-yellow niche product favored by college football players and other elite athletes. Now sports drinks are a multimillion-dollar business, with a rainbow of colors and flavors drunk by anyone and everyone.

Maybe glow-in-the-dark bicycles will enjoy the same rise in popularity. Maybe years from now everyone will be pedaling bikes that glow or even blink in the dark. They might become a huge part of the bicycle business, and people will be saying, "Yeah, a professor and two students came up with the idea at the University of Florida back in 2001."

Christopher Niezrecki sure hopes so. He's the mechanical engineering professor who encouraged Greg Yoder and Matthew Young to develop a bike that made cyclists much more visible at night. Rather than merely adding lights and reflectors, the two used electroluminescent strips to line the bike frame and tire rims.

The glow strips, powered by nine-volt batteries, turn bicycles into rolling light shows. Motorists can see the bikes from up to 600 feet away, and Yoder says some hoot and holler at the rare sight of one gleaming in the dark.

The Florida professor and his students developed the project with a $16,000 grant from the National Collegiate Inventors and Innovators Alliance. A prototype was demonstrated at a Las Vegas trade show, with the university seeking companies to license the bicycle. Now they're all waiting and hoping for glow-in-the-dark bikes to light up an entire industry.

Just like Gatorade.

B OGEYS   UNDER   THE   L IGHTS
Gainesville

I t's not necessary to travel to Alaska if you want to play golf at midnight. The opportunity is available at Gainesville's West End Golf Club, advertised as the "World's Largest Lighted Golf Course."

How do they know this to be true? "*Golf Digest* did an article saying we were the largest lighted golf course in the world and nobody disputed it," said club employee Stan Mitchell.

So there you have it.

Open since 1968, West End is 3,940 yards long and plays to a par of sixty. There are six par fours, the longest a formidable 430-yarder, and twelve par threes ranging from 135 yards to 188 yards. The course record is fifty-three, shot by head pro Scott Dombek.

You can play the course by day, if you wish, but to get the true West End experience, you have to tee it up after the sun goes down. The lights give the terrain an eerie quality and also cast some distracting shadows. The tees and greens are well-lighted, but there are some dark spots if you veer too far from the fairway on the longer holes.

The word at West End is, if you're going to slice it, slice it next to one of the light poles. You get a free drop if they impede your swing.

Besides being relatively cheap (you can walk the course for $12), West End is also a great way to beat the summer heat. Just remember to pay attention to the golfers around you. Golf balls hurt just as much at night as they do during the day.

The West End Golf Club is located 3½ miles west of I–75 on State Road 26. The course is open from 7:30 A.M. to midnight. During the winter months, the course is closed at night on weekends. For more information, call (352) 332–2721 or visit the Web site www.westend.com.

GATORS LOVE THEIR BURRITO BROTHERS
Gainesville

For University of Florida alumni, there's nothing like returning to campus for a Saturday night football game. It's a chance to wear orange and blue, sing "We Are the Boys of Old Florida," and eat at Burrito Brothers, a Gainesville institution for twenty-six years. On some nights, the wait in line—for takeout, mind you—can be more than an hour.

For Gators who can't make it to Gainesville, the restaurant ships frozen burritos as far as California and Hawaii.

"We do a lot of orders for Gator Clubs around the Southeast," says Randy Akerson, who founded the restaurant with his wife, Janet. "We send a huge order to Chicago every year. It's mind-boggling."

Janet's a former English major; Randy dropped out of the UF law school after injuring his back. While working at a nearby sub shop, he got an offer to start a little Mexican restaurant just across the street from campus. The place took its name from a 1970s country-rock group, The Flying Burrito Brothers.

"When I started in Gainesville, there were only two or three Mexican restaurants, including the large chain I won't name," Randy says. "Now there's much more traffic and much more competition. We haven't changed, though, and that gives us a little romantic cachet."

Black bean and pinto bean burritos and tacos are on the menu, along with fresh homemade salsa and guacamole. Nothing fancy, nothing expensive. The place has never expanded, never franchised, and never lost the hole-in-the-wall charm that made it a success in the first place.

Out front is a Latin inscription, appropriate for a university town restaurant. And what wisdom does Burrito Brothers offers its learned customers? "Oh," says Randy, laughing. "It says, 'Please ask for sauce when ordering.'"

The Burrito Brothers Taco Co. is at 16 N.W. 13th Street, Gainesville. For more information, call (352) 378–5948.

THE MYSTIQUE OF DEVIL'S MILLHOPPER
Gainesville

Devil's Millhopper, Gainesville's giant sinkhole and state geological site, got its fearsome name from Florida settlers in the nineteenth century. They compared the shape of the hole to the funnel of a gristmill that fed flour into a grinder. Only this earthen mill apparently fed bodies to the devil. Why else would there be fossilized bones and teeth at the bottom?

Pretty good PR for what amounts to a hole in the ground, 120 feet deep and 500 feet across.

Devil's Millhopper became a destination for early Florida train travelers, with picture postcards of the site dating back to 1906. Erosion took its toll before the state bought the sixty-two-acre site in 1974. Park workers built a wooden staircase to help prevent erosion and maintain a lush landscape nourished by spring-fed waterfalls.

What captured the imagination of early settlers now soothes the souls of late-afternoon visitors.

Devil's Millhopper State Geological Site is at 4732 Millhopper Road, Gainesville. For more information, call (352) 955–2008.

THE DEVIL MADE ME DO IT
Inglis

f you come to Inglis for the purpose of meeting Satan, you're in for a let down.

Mayor Carolyn Risher banished Satan from Inglis in the fall of 2001. If you doubt the truth of this, there are five copies of an official, signed, sealed city proclamation attesting to the fact. One is on Mayor Risher's office wall, between the Elvis paintings and a depiction of the Last Supper. The other four are in hollowed-out fence posts next to the four main roads leading into the city. The posts are painted with the words *Repent, Request, and Resist.*

Mayor Risher came up with the idea of banishing Satan from Inglis on Halloween night while seated at her kitchen table. Maybe the candy ran out and things got ugly; one can never be completely sure what causes things like this.

Her explanation was that Inglis, located about 75 miles north of Tampa, was bedeviled by immoral behavior, including but not limited to drunken drivers, fathers who molest their daughters, and people who steal from their neighbors. Town Clerk Sally McCranie, who also signed the proclamation, added that some of the town's teens have taken to dressing in black and painting their faces white. For a town of 1,400, there appears to be a lot going on in Inglis.

At the time of this writing, Mayor Risher's proclamation was being assailed by the American Civil Liberties Union, some Inglis residents, and some members of the city council. By the time you read this, it is possible that Satan will have been unbanished from Inglis, which is good or bad news depending on how you feel about church-state issues and/or fifteen-year-olds dressing up like Marilyn Manson.

DEALING WITH PEOPLE WHO
CROSS THE LINE
Jennings

ourists who cross from Georgia into Florida on I–75 may
believe that they will immediately encounter an alligator,
Mickey Mouse, or a swarm of mosquitoes. Instead, they are
greeted by Patrick Burke, the manager of one of five visitor
welcome centers strung along Florida's northern boundary.
Two of his employees, Patricia Brown and Rosetta Townsend,
have sixty years of experience between them handing out complimentary cups of Florida orange juice and answering
tourists' questions that range from "How far to Disney World?"
(214 miles) to "Are alligators dangerous?" (Yes, especially if
you feed them) or "Where's the nearest nudist camp?" (The staff
keeps a file).

The offer of free orange or grapefruit juice, maps, and information draws 2.5 million visitors a year to the state's five welcome centers. At the center on I–75, just north of Jennings, the
staff pours 1,500 gallons of juice a month, four ounces at a
time. Unlike earlier days, you can have more than one serving.

To work at a Florida visitor center, you have to pass a one
hundred-question test dealing with Florida government, history, and tourist attractions, both major and minor. Besides
Disney World, tourists also ask where they can find a mock-up
of the Hanoi Hilton (Pensacola), where they can drive a real
Winston Cup race car (Orlando), and how the town of Two Egg
got its name (residents bartered eggs for other goods; two eggs
was the minimum for a trade).

Probably the most frequently asked question is whether the
visitor center gives away free or reduced-price tickets to Disney
World. (No. You have to stop at one of the Disney-affiliated

*Folks who stop at the Florida Welcome Center just south of
Georgia on I-75 can get a free cup of orange juice and
directions to the nearest nudist camp.*

tourist centers farther down the road for these.) Occasionally,
there is a mini crisis to deal with. More often than you would
like to think, visitors leave kids or pets behind. Although these
oversights are usually noticed fairly quickly, there have been
times when a husband towing a mobile home has driven away,
not realizing that his wife has gotten out of the vehicle to go to
the rest room. Sometimes it's hours before the husband realizes
anything is amiss.

The visitor welcome center on I–75 is such a popular place
that it actually became a roadside hazard. The state had to
move the WELCOME TO FLORIDA sign back off the highway

because tourists were getting out of their cars and posing to have their pictures taken. With cars and trucks whipping by at 70-plus miles per hour, there was understandable concern that someone would get killed.

But today, the visitor center is just a friendly place to stop, have a cup of juice, and maybe ask directions.

"Is this a fresh map?" an elderly lady in sunglasses asks. "Yes, ma'am," answers Patricia Brown, trying not to roll her eyes. "It's the freshest one we've got."

SWAN LAKE
Lakeland

There is no record of Richard the Lionhearted ever having visited Lakeland, but his name is connected with this mid-Florida city just the same.

What the two have in common is swans. About 800 years ago, Richard, who was involved with the Crusades, received a pair of white mute swans from Queen Beatrice of Cypress. (Today, she would probably have just sent him a bunch of mylar balloons spelling out "Best of luck!")

Fast forward to 1956. Lakeland, whose ten major lakes had been home to a varying number of the graceful birds since at least 1923, saw its last swan fall victim to an alligator in 1954. Mrs. Robert Pickhardt, a Lakeland native living in England at the time, was familiar with the royal flock of swans on the Thames—birds descended from the original pair given to Richard, he of the lion heart. She inquired about purchasing a pair for Lakeland. Queen Elizabeth, known to be a little tight with a farthing, agreed to send a pair of swans to Lakeland if the city would pay the cost of capture, crating, and shipping, estimated at $300.

Eventually the money was raised, and a pair of white mute swans from England were released on Lake Morton on February 9, 1957. Descendants of that pair continue to grace the city's many lakes; today there are more than 200 birds, including white mutes, Australian black swans, white Coscorba swans from the Falkland Islands, black-neck swans from South America, white pelicans, ducks, geese, and other species.

Lakeland has learned its lesson and is very protective of its swans now. There is an annual swan round-up, at which time the graceful birds are inoculated against disease, and the city provides feeding stations and breeding pens along Lake Morton's perimeter. An S-necked swan is now the city's official logo, and a few years ago a swan postage stamp was issued out of respect for the bird's place in the city's history.

A good place to view the swans of Lake Morton is at the corner of Lake Morton Drive and East Palmetto Avenue, near the Lakeland Library. If you're driving, be careful; the swans have the right-of-way.

A LAND BRIDGE ACROSS I-75
Ocala

From Interstate 75, it looks like any other overpass in Florida. From the seat of a bike or a horse, though, the Cross Florida Greenway land bridge is something else: a trail link, the shape of things to come, and a defiant step against the tyranny of interstate traffic.

Local advocates call the land bridge the first of its kind in the United States. The $3.4 million overpass is 52 feet wide and 200 feet long, following a natural ridge across the interstate about 9 miles south of Ocala. The specially designed supports carry fieldstone walls, tons of topsoil, and irrigated planters with oaks, pines, and native vegetation.

"This bridge is the bridge of the twenty-first century," said David Struhs, secretary for the Department of Environmental Protection (DEP), at the 2000 grand opening. "It will connect 15 miles of biking trails, 56 miles of equestrian trails, and 40 miles of hiking trails, but this bridge will also reconnect Floridians back to the land and will connect us to our new future."

The land bridge also allows small animals—foxes, raccoons, and possums—to cross what had been a busy barrier of traffic along I–75. As of yet, local animals haven't left any signs, but it's easy to imagine wildlife graffiti: "I brake for bipeds." "My cub is an honor student in the Ocala National Forest." "If this tree is a-rockin', don't come a-knockin'."

Back in the real world, the land bridge has managed to bring together hikers, bikers, and horsemen, groups traditionally at odds with one another. Kenneth Smith, the local section head for the Florida Trail Association, was presented with a DEP plaque honoring that cooperation.

"We can't stop the interstates; they're part of our lives," he said. "But we can't let them stop us, either."

The Ocala land bridge crosses I–75 north, north of exit 67. The nearest trailhead is east of the interstate on County Road 475A in Belleview. For more information, contact the Office of Greenways and Trails, 8282 S.E. County Road 314, Ocala. Phone (352) 236–7143.

WHAT A DRAG
Ocala

At the "Big Daddy" Don Garlits Museum of Drag Racing, you might actually run into the "Swamp Rat" himself. The seventy-year-old legend and his wife, Pat, live in a house on the grounds, and it's not unusual for him to stop by the

museum, chat with visitors, and maybe share a story or two
about what it was like to cover a quarter mile in 4.72 seconds
at a top speed of 303.27 miles per hour.

Garlits is clear on the details because he did it only a year
ago, at the age of sixty-nine, at the Indianapolis Speedway. It
was his own personal lifetime speed record, which is pretty
remarkable for a man who has been racing cars for more than
half a century and has won just about every trophy and award
the sport can bestow.

While other men his age contemplate their next nap or a few
vigorous hands of bridge, Garlits continues to tinker with
dragsters, occasionally racing them. He does this despite suffering near-fatal burns in a 1959 accident in Chester, South
Carolina, and losing half his right foot when a transmission
exploded in 1969.

Garlits, by the way, was given his nickname by his daughters, who used to watch him from the stands while shouting,
"Go, daddy! Go, daddy! Go, daddy!" A track announcer modified the chant and began calling him Big Daddy, which is bit of
a joke because he stands no taller than five-nine.

The museum, which Garlits opened in 1983, contains about
150 drag racers with names like *Pandemonium, Pollutionizer,
Bounty Hunter,* and *Yellow Fang.* Garlits's cars, painted in
trademark black, include *Swamp Rat 22,* the famous dragster
that set the 1975 world speed record (250.69 miles per hour in
5.63 seconds) that stood for seven years. Nearby is *Swamp Rat
27,* a 1981 model that was powered by a supercharged, fuel-
injected, 454-cubic-inch Dodge Hemi engine that generated
2,700 horsepower and could cover the quarter-mile track in
6.20 seconds at a top speed of 230 miles per hour. The car
burned "nitro," which is short for nitromethane. You never
hear drag racers complain about the price of unleaded regular;
a gallon of nitro goes for $40.

Garlits is credited with many innovations in drag racing,
including the rear-mounted engine, bicycle tires on the front,

and driver canopies. Called the King of the Dragsters, Garlits set numerous speed records and has won 144 national events and 17 world titles.

At the museum, it's rather odd to see all that power sitting in front of you, not moving. Drag racing is all about flames and smoking tires and ear-splitting noise. The cars on display here are as quiet as extinct dinosaurs. But if you're a fan of drag racing, none of that will matter. The exhibits will bring back memories of great cars and the men who raced them.

For those who prefer slower, quieter vehicles, there is a Classic Car Collection next door to the drag racing museum. Cars from the early 1900s to the present are on display, including flathead Fords, a 1956 Chrysler sedan that once belonged to former President Eisenhower, a 1950 Mercury that was once driven by "The Fonz" on the television show *Happy Days,* and a 1904 Orient Buckboard. Built mostly of wood, the Buckboard, at $375, was advertised as the "Cheapest Automobile in the World."

If you're not lucky enough to run into Big Daddy at his museum (we weren't), there's a good chance you'll meet Billy or Baby Doll, Garlits's two Yorkies who hang out in the gift shop. (Be advised that Baby Doll is very much the friendlier of the two.)

We passed on the T-shirts and ball caps, but we did dip into a box of grapefruits sitting by the door. The hand-lettered sign said they were from the Swamp Rat's own tree and were free for the taking.

So we did.

The Museum of Drag Racing is located south of Ocala at 13700 S.W. 16th Avenue, just off I-75 exit 67. The museum and the Classic Car Collection are open daily from 9:00 A.M. to 5:00 P.M. Admission is $12.00 for adults, $10.00 for seniors 55 and older, $10.00 for ages thirteen to eighteen, and $3.00 for ages five to twelve. For more information, call (352) 245-8661 or visit the Web site www.garlits.com.

Go, Fighting Sandcrabs!

*F*lorida high schools have
their share of Gators,
Seminoles, and Hurricanes, following the traditions of state university athletic teams. There are
also plenty of Lions, Tigers, and
Bears—oh, my!—along with the usual
Eagles, Wildcats, and Bulldogs.

Other schools are more creative, more
original, when it comes to school mascots
and nicknames.

Apopka High School features the Blue
Darters, and at Admiral Farragut Academy
in St. Petersburg, the players are Bluejackets,
after the Union naval officer who stormed
Mobile Bay during the Civil War.

Then there's the All Saints' Academy in Winter Haven.
Yep, they're the Saints. The All Saints' Saints. The best play-
ers could form a team called The All Saints' All-Stars, or
The All-Stars All Saints . . . something like that.

Nautical names float from the Gulf of Mexico to the
Atlantic Ocean. There are the Charlotte High School Tarpons
and the Coral Reef High School Barracudas. At Cocoa
Beach High School, boys' and girls' teams are known simply
as "The Beach." The Key West Conchs are named after a
local seashell. Then there are the Lakeland Dreadnaughts,
the Mariner Tritons, the Miami Beach Hi-Tides, the Miami
Senior High Stingarees, and the Seabreeze High School
Fighting Sandcrabs.

Father Lopez High School in Daytona Beach offers the Greenwaves. In Tallahassee, there are the Florida A&M Developmental School Baby Rattlers and Rattlerettes. Fort Lauderdale High School has the Flying L's. At Hialeah High School, near the famous racetrack, teams are the Thoroughbreds.

Then there are the Hilliard High School Flashes, the Howard Middle School Bumblebees and Lady Bumblebees, and the Laurel Hill High School Hoboes. Okeechobee High School offers the Brahmans. Osceola High has its Kowboys with a K. We have the Poplar Springs Atomics and the Tarpon Springs High School Spongers, after the local sponge-diving industry.

The Broward Christian School is diplomatic; they're the Ambassadors. Chiefland High School has the Indians—no surprise there. And Dixie M. Hollins High in St. Petersburg? The Rebels, of course.

BURGERS, SHAKES, AND HISTORY TOO
Palatka

You know you're in a genuine Southern diner if the first question the waitress asks you when you plop down on a counter stool is, "Sweet tea, hon?"

Angels Diner, Florida's oldest, still does things pretty much the same way it's been doing them since it opened in 1932. You can still order a pusalow—made with chocolate milk, vanilla syrup, and crushed ice—or a black bottom sandwich, which consists of bacon, scrambled eggs, and hamburger mixed together, grilled, and served on a bun.

Fashioned from an old railroad dining car, Angels has only ten counter stools and six tables, so the place fills up quickly. Overflow crowds can order curb service and sit at one of several picnic tables situated in the parking lot under a sheet metal overhang.

Angels, a local dining institution, is also popular with college kids headed off to St. Augustine Beach. Founded by Porter Angel and now owned by the Browning family, the diner is a must-stop for politicians campaigning in the area. Governor Jeb Bush had a bite to eat at Angels during his last campaign. (None of the waitresses could remember what he ordered, let alone what he said.)

"The place gets in your blood," says manager Martha Gocio, who has worked at Angels for the past seventeen years. She is presumably referring to tradition, not cholesterol, of which there is plenty on the Angels menu. The cheeseburgers ($1.99) and fried onion rings ($1.70) were so good our chests hurt just thinking about them.

A diner is nothing without nostalgia, and Angels has plenty, starting with the metal stairs leading up to the narrow door, passing by the trays on the wall urging you to drink Coca-Cola in bottles for 5 cents, and ending with the jukebox, where Fats

Angels Diner, Florida's oldest, occupies an old dining car in downtown Palatka. There's plenty of nostalgia and the pusalows are to die for.

Domino, the Andrew Sisters, and Elvis compete for airtime with Supertramp.

About the only concessions Angels has made to the passing of time are a NO SMOKING sign next to the two tables by the door, and an air-conditioning system, the ductwork of which fits in nicely with the general diner decor.

As Martha Gocio said, the place gets in your blood.

More sweet tea, please, ma'am, and pass the ketchup.

Angels Diner is located at 209 Reid Street next to the Subway. It's open 6:00 A.M. to 11:00 P.M. Sunday through Thursday, and 6:00 A.M. to 2:00 A.M. Friday and Saturday. The diner is closed on Christmas. Phone (904) 325–3927.

THE NAZI INVASION OF FLORIDA
Pointe Vedra Beach

After the infamous September 11, 2001, attack on the United States, President George W. Bush authorized the use of military tribunals to try accused members of the al-Qaida network of terrorists. This legal tactic was controversial, but the Bush administration argued there was a direct precedent: when Nazi saboteurs landed in Florida during World War II.

Most present-day Floridians greeted this news with the same reaction: Say what?

Yet it was true, in a little-remembered incident of the great conflict. During June 1942, just six months after the surprise attack on Pearl Harbor brought the United States into the war, eight German spies slipped into the country. Nazi submarines dropped four of them off on Long Island, New York, and another four on Pointe Vedra Beach south of Jacksonville. The Germans in Florida landed in naval uniforms, then changed into civilian clothes, burying their uniforms and sabotage equipment in the sand.

(In case you ever have to play a particularly brutal level of Trivial Pursuit, Florida Edition, those Germans were Edward John Kerling, 33; Werner Thiel, 35; Herman Otto Neubauer, 32; and Herbert Hans Haupt, 22.)

The Nazi spies, who had all lived in the United States, took a bus to Jacksonville and then went by train to Cincinnati. One pair went to Chicago; the others continued to New York City. They carried more than $170,000 in cash, along with lists of contacts and targets that included department stores. The spies were betrayed by George Johann Dasch, one of those who landed on Long Island, and soon all eight were captured. Six were executed.

Michael Gannon, a history professor at the University of Florida, told the Associated Press that the saboteurs were not important. "They accomplished nothing. They were captured right away," he said. "These people truly were inconsequential, but they have piqued the American imagination."

That assessment might be a bit of a stretch. There's no historical marker commemorating the event, and locals and visitors don't think much of Nazi saboteurs, military tribunals, or the summer of '42.

Footnotes of history apparently last no longer than footprints in the sand.

ROMEO, ROMEO! WHEREFORE ART THOU, ROMEO?
Romeo

Finding Romeo is easy. Take State Road 40 west from Ocala, through Martel, then bear right onto County Road 328, go about 10 miles, and you're there.

Romeo is little more than a sign on the road and nearby Juliette is no more. Hey, many of Shakespeare's plays had sad endings too.

Trouble is, there's not much "there" to Romeo. Just a couple of signs on US 41 telling you you're entering and leaving the place. It would be just another farming community were it not for its moniker. Founded in 1850, Romeo got its name because it was just 10 miles north of Juliette. What do you think they were going to call the place? Iago?

Just like her star-crossed Shakespearean character, Juliette is no longer around. What was once Juliette is now Rainbow Springs State Park. Her name, however, lives on at Rainbow Springs Country Club, which named its restaurant after Romeo's lover.

We hear the Capulet burgers are to die for.

EXCUSE ME, SIR, I MISTOOK YOU FOR A GHOST
St. Augustine

omeowners in St. Augustine don't brag about their new kitchens, fancy wallpaper, or high-tech TVs. They know the only sure way to impress their friends and neighbors is to boast that your home has a ghost.

To hear people talk, there are almost as many unliving walking around here as there are living. That could stem from the fact that St. Augustine, founded in 1565, is the oldest continuously occupied city in America. Over the years, the French, the Spanish, and the English have laid claim to St. Augustine, leaving behind a rich loam of international intrigue from which ghosts love to spring.

We bought a copy of *A Ghostly Experience: Tales of Saint Augustine Florida* at the bookstore next to the Oldest House, and the cashier immediately asked if we had had any personal experiences with the undead. (We haven't.) Then he went off on a long and rather predictable story about the strange noises that came from the unoccupied apartment above him, and how they only happened at night, and how he never identified their source, etc., etc. Pretty soon another cashier is chiming in about her supernatural encounter and we're still waiting for our change and it's getting late and we still haven't had any lunch.

The point of all this being that it is not hard to get the residents of St. Augustine to talk about ghosts.

But the most efficient way to learn about the city's things that go bump in the night is to take the "Ghostly Experience" Walking Tour. The tour begins at 8:00 P.M. nightly next to the Oldest Wooden Schoolhouse (everything in St. Augustine is the oldest something-or-other) and lasts an hour and a half. During that time, a guide dressed in a monk's robe or some other "period" outfit leads a group of fifteen or so down some of the city's dark, narrow streets, past cemeteries and old houses that no self-respecting haunt could pass up.

Our guide, Michael, halted us beside the St. Francis Inn at 279 St. George Street. (St. George Street, by the way, is like an interstate highway for ghosts. It looks like something straight out of a Harry Potter book.) Then he told us the story of the nephew of a military officer who fell in love with one of the house servants in the middle part of the nineteenth century. The couple would sneak up into the attic (now room 3-A) to, as Michael says with a wink, "hold hands." The uncle discovered them and furiously sent the servant away, instructing his nephew that he was never to see her again.

Broken-hearted, the nephew hanged himself in the attic.

Today, it is believed that the ghost of the young servant, named Lily, has taken up residence in room 3-A. While cleaning the room, a housekeeper turned on the TV to keep her company. She went out to the hallway to get some bed linens and when she returned, the TV was switched off.

The housekeeper's line, allegedly, was that "Lily doesn't like MTV."

If you think tourists would go out of their way to avoid staying in room 3-A, you don't understand the "spirit" of St. Augustine. Reservations are booked a year in advance, and some tourists refuse to leave until they see an apparition or a piece of furniture moving by itself.

They not only ain't afraid of no ghosts in St. Augustine, most places are accepting applications.

The Ghost Tour meets by the Oldest Wooden Schoolhouse at 8:00 P.M. every night except Memorial Day and Labor Day. Tickets are $8.00 for adults; free for children under six. Phone (904) 461–1009 or (888) 461–1009.

SHE LOVES ME, SHE LOVES ME KNOT
St. Augustine

On Orange Street, near the intersection of Cordova Street, is a strange thing of the botanical kind.

In the front yard of a private residence, a palm tree is growing out of the trunk of an oak tree. Both trees are full-grown and appear quite healthy, or at least as healthy as something can appear that has another thing growing out of its body.

The legend of St. Augustine's Love Tree is more romantic than the reality, which basically consists of one tree strangling another.

Perhaps because they are intertwined so inextricably, the duo is called the Love Tree. Legend has it that if a guy and a gal kiss in the shadow of the Love Tree, they will be frozen in a tomb of wood forever with birds pooping on their heads and termites gnawing on their hindquarters.

Wait. That's a different legend. Ah, yes. This legend says that the kissing couple will remain in love to their dying day.

Or until someone cuts the Love Tree down to make room for a condo, whichever comes first.

*T*HIS *R*EALLY *O*LD *H*OUSE
St. Augustine

There are only two things wrong with the Gonzalez-Alvarez House's claim to be the Oldest House:

1. No one knows exactly how old it is.
2. It's not the Oldest House.

What the building at 14 St. Francis Street is is (probably) the oldest continuously occupied house in the oldest continuously occupied city in America. Our tour guide pointed out that some houses in New England are older, as is an adobe hut in New Mexico.

But these are nothing more than annoying quibbles in a town that boasts of not only having the Oldest House, but also the Oldest Wooden Schoolhouse and the Oldest Drug Store. (We stayed in a motel that quite possibly had the Oldest Plumbing, but that claim has not yet been authenticated.)

Still, there is no doubt that the Oldest House is very, very old. Archaeologists claim that some sort of building has been continuously occupied on the Oldest House site since the early 1600s.

The building at 14 St. Francis Street in St. Augustine is believed to be the oldest house in the United States by everyone except those who say it isn't.

The building that tourists visit today is the same, more or less, as the building that was rebuilt after British troops burned St. Augustine to the ground for the second time in 1702.

A modern real estate agent would probably describe the Oldest House as a "fixer-upper." The original bottom floor consisted of two rooms in which eight people lived. There was no glass in the windows (too expensive), and a brazier in the middle of the floor of the main room was kept continuously stoked—in the winter to provide heat and in the summer to smoke away mosquitoes. Bedding consisted of a thin straw mat unfurled over a floor of tabby, a concretelike mixture of lime, shell, and sand.

Our guide said that the house was typical of how the "upper middle class" lived in St. Augustine in the early 1700s. Those less well off presumably stayed in our motel.

One of the earliest known occupants of the Oldest House was Tomas Gonzalez y Hernandez, an artilleryman at the nearby fort. When Spain ceded Florida to England in 1763, the town's 3,000 Spanish residents, including Gonzalez and his family, had to leave.

The house changed hands several times and was eventually bought at auction in 1790 by Geronimo Alvarez. He and his descendants lived in the house for more than one hundred years, adding a second story and furnishings that look positively modern compared to what's going on on the floor below.

The Oldest House, like just about every other building in St. Augustine built before 1980, is said to be haunted by ghosts. We didn't meet any, but we didn't volunteer to spend the night either.

The Oldest House is located at 14 St. Francis Street near the Charlotte Street intersection. Next to it is the Tovar House, another extremely old house, and a military museum that displays weapons dating back hundreds of years. For more information, call (904) 824-2872 or visit the Web site www.oldcity.com/oldhouse/.

LAND OF 1,000 GATORS
St. Augustine

There are no roller coasters at St. Augustine Alligator Farm Zoological Park, nor any plummeting elevators or things that spin you around until you lose your lunch.

The place is basically about alligators. Lots of alligators. More than 1,000 of them and their crocodile cousins. The biggest is Baby Huey, a 13-foot gator that weighs more than 900 pounds. Baby Huey doesn't put on much of a show. In fact, he mostly just lies there, soaking up the sun and looking dead. You, as a tourist, are supposed to look at Baby Huey and say, "Whoa! That is one big gator! Do you think it's alive?"

That was about all the entertainment value visitors used to need or expect from Florida tourist attractions before the D-word arrived in Orlando and changed everything. The Alligator Farm, one of Florida's oldest tourist attractions, has been in operation since the early 1890s. The fact that it's still around testifies to the fact that some people still prefer a real, if somnambulant, gator to a hyperactive animatronic mouse.

The pens and ponds in which the gators live give off a swampy smell, another clue that you are not in the land of the plastic rodent. This is not to say that the Alligator Farm does not have a sense of whimsy. On an island on which numerous 10-foot alligators roam is a sign that reads NO TRESPASSING! Understandably, the attraction doesn't find it necessary to post guards to keep people from jumping the fence.

There are other interesting critters at the park besides alligators and crocodiles. We particularly enjoyed the Galapagos tortoises, which can live to be 200 years old and weigh more than 600 pounds. Looking like reptilian Volkswagens, the tor-

A No Trespassing sign seems unnecessary to discourage tourists from climbing into the alligator pit at the Alligator Farm Zoological Park in St. Augustine.

toises lumber along, munching grass and lettuce given them by their keepers. Compared to the gators and crocs, these guys seem like roadrunners.

The best time to visit the Alligator Farm is in the late afternoon when flocks of blue herons, white egrets, ibis, and wood storks return from a day of feeding to the rookery at the attraction. When we visited, in March, the egrets were decked out in their mating plumage, lacy white tail feathers that hunters used to collect for women's hats, bringing the species to the verge of extinction.

Also, don't miss the show at the Reptile Theater where handler Shannon Chapman will let you pet her friend, Chip the alligator.

No need to be afraid. Chip's mouth is taped shut.

With Scotch tape.

The Alligator Farm Zoological Park is located on State Road A1A just across the Bridge of Lions from St. Augustine. The park is open daily from 9:00 A.M. to 6:00 P.M. Phone (904) 824–3337 for more information. Admission is charged.

GOMEK THE MAGNIFICENT

O*nce upon a time, a long time ago, there was born in New Guinea a little crocodile by the name of . . .*

Actually, the little crocodile didn't have a name because it was . . . well, little. But the little crocodile grew and grew and grew until it was very big and it started eating natives the way you or I might eat popcorn shrimp at Red Lobster. Local villagers gave the big croc a name. They called it "Crocodile You Don't Want to Let in Your Restaurant on All-You-Can-Eat-Natives Fridays." No, we're making that up. They called the critter Louma, "crocodile inhabited by evil spirits."

In 1968 a trapper by the name of George Craig captured Louma. At 17½ feet and 2,000 pounds, he was proclaimed the largest crocodile in captivity. Louma, for reasons that are not entirely clear, was renamed Gomek, after an Australian comic book character. Presumably the name "Charlie Brown" was already taken.

Anyway, Gomek spent some time wowing crowds in Australia and Indonesia before winding up at the St. Augustine Alligator Farm in 1989. It didn't

take long for Gomek to become the attraction's Celebrity Croc. Gomek had his own (large) pool at the Alligator Farm and chose from a daily menu that included mullet, chicken, and smaller crocs too slow or too stupid to stay out of his way. Despite his ferocious reputation, Gomek's handlers described the huge Indopacific crocodile as docile and a good husband, in the sense that in the eight years he was at the alligator farm, he never once devoured his crocodile mate, Anna Bell.

Alas, the soft life proved Gomek's undoing; he died in 1997 of a heart attack, presumably from failing to remove the skin from his chicken.

But Gomek lives on, at least in taxidermy heaven. His enormous stuffed carcass is ensconced in its own shrinelike house on the grounds of the Alligator Farm. Believed to have been between sixty and eighty years old at the time of his death, Gomek is posed in a decidedly undocile stance, with his huge mouth agape and his feet ready to run down the most uncooperative chicken and/or villager.

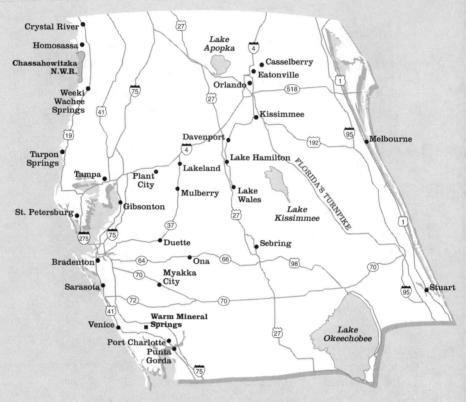

Crystal River

Homosassa

Chassahowitzka
N.W.R.

Weeki
Wachee
Springs

Tarpon
Springs

Tampa

St. Petersburg

Bradenton

Sarasota

Venice

Port Charlotte
Punta
Gorda

Plant
City

Gibsonton

Duette

Myakka
City

Warm Mineral
Springs

Lake
Apopka

Casselberry
Eatonville

Orlando

Kissimmee

Davenport

Lakeland

Mulberry

Lake Hamilton

Lake
Wales

Lake
Kissimmee

Sebring

Ona

Melbourne

Stuart

Lake
Okeechobee

FLORIDA'S TURNPIKE

27

4

518

192

95

1

1

95

70

98

66

70

72

41

64

70

37

27

27

75

19

41

275

75

CENTRAL FLORIDA

CENTRAL FLORIDA

THE BEST ARGUMENT AGAINST VEGETARIANISM YET
Bradenton

What's old and gray and likes to float nude on his back in his swimming pool while women rub his belly and feed him bite-size chunks of fruit?

No, not Hugh Hefner (but that's a good guess). It's Snooty the manatee, the official mascot and namesake of Manatee County. At fifty-four, Snooty is the oldest living manatee born in captivity. A lifelong bachelor, Snooty cruises (cavorts would be too strong a word at his age) around the 60,000-gallon Parker Aquarium in the South Florida Museum in downtown Bradenton.

Snooty maintains his svelte 1,000-pound figure by adhering to a strict vegetarian diet. Lettuce, carrots, and apples disappear into his whiskered snout at the rate of eighty pounds a day. He is also partial to sweet potatoes, broccoli, strawberries, and monkey chow. (No word on whether monkeys enjoy a snack of manatee chow.)

Snooty's handler, Carol Audette, caters to Snooty's every need, including the aforementioned belly rubs and back scrubs. Thousands of schoolchildren troop through the aquarium every year for Snooty's birthday party and to learn more about this endangered species.

With a face only a mother manatee could love, Snooty,
at fifty-four, is the oldest living captive manatee.

Wildlife experts estimate there are only about 2,500 manatees in Florida waters, and more than 200 die every year, chiefly from injuries suffered from boat propellers.

Although Snooty is definitely a tourist attraction who loves playing to the crowds, he also serves a valuable educational purpose. The children who fall in love with the docile mammal are the same children who will tell their parents to slow down their boats in waters known to contain manatees.

(Snooty's public relations value skyrocketed when someone had the good sense to change his original name, which was Stinky, and to trademark his new name.)

If you visit Snooty, don't be surprised if he has a pool mate. Injured or orphaned manatees sometimes spend a few months at the Parker Aquarium before being reintroduced to the wild. Snooty, however, isn't going anywhere. After all, monkey chow doesn't grow on trees.

The Parker Aquarium is located at 201 Tenth Street, Bradenton. The phone number is (941) 746–4131. Admission is $7.50 for adults, $6.00 for seniors, $5.00 for students, $4.00 for children five through twelve, and free for children under five accompanied by an adult. Aquarium hours are 10:00 A.M. to 5:00 P.M. Tuesday through Saturday, and noon to 5:00 P.M. on Sunday. From January through April, the aquarium is open seven days a week.

MACBETH IN THE BUFF
Casselberry

There are lots of strip clubs in Florida, but only one that offers "Macbeth in the buff." That would be Club Juana in Casselberry, north of Orlando, where club owner Michael Pinter found a loopy loophole in a 1998 Seminole County public decency ordinance. The law allowed nudity in "bona fide performances" of "legitimate theater," so Club Juana laid the bard bare with a nightclub act of nude Shakespeare.

Local headlines on the controversy included "Hubba, Hubba, Toil and Trouble."

Nude performers acted out the witches scene of Macbeth, along with a Marquis de Sade routine called "Politics in the Bedroom" and a sketch that's a tribute to the Web, "Cyberotica." Lt. Sammy Gibson of the county investigative bureau attended the performance for legal review. His report described

*At Club Juana in Casselberry, dancers skirt local nudity
ordinances by incorporating "legitimate theater" into their acts. Or
as the local headlines put it: "Hubba, Hubba, Toil and Trouble."*

"some choreography to it and some reading parts and speech
parts and literature parts."

Elizabeth Maupin, the *Orlando Sentinel* theater critic,
reviewed a videotape of the Club Juana performance. Her opinion: "Let me just say that if there was a crime committed here,
it wasn't against the nudity ordinance."

In spite of poor theatrical reviews, the nude routine remains
popular with paying customers at Club Juana. The long-
running "Macbeth" still tops the marquee.

WHOOP! THERE IT IS!
Crystal River

If you looked up at the sky above Chassahowitzka National
Wildlife Refuge last fall, you might have thought to yourself:
Wow! That's one hard-to-pronounce national wildlife refuge!

But that would have been stupid. What you should have
thought was that you were witnessing a scene out of the movie
Fly Away Home.

A flock of large birds, flying in formation, was gamely following an ultralight airplane piloted by a guy in a white suit.
The birds were whooping cranes, eight of 'em, and they were
on the last leg of a 1,300-mile journey that began at Necedah
National Wildlife Refuge in Wisconsin.

The odd procession was the first step in building what will
hopefully be the first self-sustaining colony of whoopers in
Florida and the second in the nation. In the 1940s, due to over-
hunting and loss of habitat, only fifteen birds remained. Life
got better for North America's largest bird when then-President
Franklin D. Roosevelt created the Aransas National Wildlife
Refuge out of 47,000 acres of marsh and forest in Texas. That
colony now consists of more than 150 whoopers. (Can you tell
we love using the word *whoopers?*)

Scientists discovered that whooping cranes lay two eggs
each year, but only one survives. That allowed them to take one
egg from each nest and artificially hatch it. The only problem
was that there were no adult whoopers around to lead the
young birds south for the winter.

That's when the idea of the ultralight airplane was born. The
chicks' keepers, wearing white jumpsuits so as to resemble
(sort of) momma, played recordings of the airplane's propeller

noise to the babies before they hatched. When born, the chicks were not afraid of the airplanes and were willing to follow them into the air.

Why ultralights? They're the only aircraft that can fly slow enough—about 35 miles per hour—for the cranes to keep up.

Even so, the flight south was no day in the swamp. The birds and their gas-powered mother averaged only 30 miles a day, and storms were frequent. Two of the eight birds were lost in a windstorm; another was killed by a bobcat shortly after arrival.

The birds, only seven months old when they arrived at the 30,000-acre Chassahowitzka Refuge, are free to come and go as they please, leaving open the possibility of more losses. They seem to be comfortable in their new surroundings though, according to Chuck Underwood of the U.S. Fish and Wildlife Service, and they spend their days feasting on blue crabs, snails, and small fish.

Come spring, the whoopers will (hopefully) be able to find their way back to Wisconsin on their own, without an ultralight escort. A fresh batch of birds will be chaperoned down south every fall for the next few years until a self-sustaining breeding colony of the 5-foot-tall cranes is established.

Until then, if you look skyward at the right time of year, you might be treated to the rare sight of a flock of whooping cranes and their sputtering momma heading south for the winter.

(Whoopers, whoopers, whoopers.)

At present, the public is not allowed to get up close and personal with the whooping cranes, but that policy is expected to relax once the colony establishes itself. For more information, call the park at (352) 563–2088. The refuge's headquarters are located at 1520 S.E. Kings Bay Drive, Crystal River, and online at www.chassahowitzka.fws.gov.

HANG GLIDERS SOAR OVER WALLABY RANCH
Davenport

There are no wallabies at Wallaby Ranch. No kangaroos or koalas either, mate. There is hang gliding, though, lots of hang gliding. The sport was invented in Australia, which means it all makes sense in a soaring sort of way west of Orlando.

On a clear day, pilots can see all the way to Walt Disney World.

Wallaby Ranch is billed as the world's largest full-time hang-gliding club, but it might also be the best-kept secret in central Florida. Directions to the place lead to a mailbox—yes, a mailbox—along lonely State Road 54 near Clermont. There you'll find a tiny sign, along with a bumper sticker that reads HANG-GLIDER PILOT: I BRAKE FOR BIRDS. For owner Malcolm Jones, Wallaby Ranch is his Shangri-La, and business is just about right.

"It's mostly word of mouth," he says. "You don't see blinking lights out there. We're not trying to be Gatorland. It's sort of a commune we have here. We live here; this is our home.

"It's like our little oasis of hang-gliding hippiedom," Jones explains. "It actually isn't as hippie as it used to be, when everything was cheaper, but the camaraderie's quick and strong."

Hang gliding is usually associated with mountains, where pilots can launch off cliffs, but Wallaby Ranch was one of the pioneers in aero-towing, using ultralight airplanes to tow gliders into the sky. The wry "Fine Print" section of the Wallaby Ranch brochure includes a cross section of slogans, advice, and philosophies of life for visiting pilots:

"Have fun, relax. Be cool, get a T-shirt. Stay upwind. Don't land in the orange grove next door. No whiners! Try to remember to pay—sometimes we forget to ask. Remember that we are a club, not an industry. Share in the positive energy of the Ranch lifestyle. Peace."

After a visit to Australia, Jones decided to name his Florida camp for the cuddly Australian animal. It was more of a personal than a business decision.

"I didn't want to call it the ABC Flight Center, you know?" he says. "Originally, I wanted to have wallabies out here."

That plan ended when it turned out that the animals are scared to death—literally—of dogs. They would have had to be kept in a walled cage that kind of defeated the purpose of the whole idea.

There is hang gliding at Wallaby Ranch, though, lots of hang gliding.

Wallaby Ranch is at 1805 Dean Still Road, Davenport 33837. Tandem discovery flights are $75. Student certification packages, glider rentals, and flying club rates are also offered. Cabins are $15.00 a night; tent sites are $5.00. For more information, visit www.wallaby.com or call (863) 424–0070.

DON'T TALK, JUST DUETTE
Duette

One might quibble whether it's actually a one-room schoolhouse (a classroom and an adjoining auditorium/lunchroom are connected by a door), but Duette Elementary is unquestionably Florida's last one-teacher schoolhouse.

For many years, that teacher has been Donna King, or "Miss Donna" as she's lovingly known to her students, who until recently numbered about fifteen. But with Manatee County's

population continually pushing eastward, the little school that
could was bursting with twenty-nine students during the
2001–2002 school year. (For the first time, a teacher assistant,
Judy Coker, was assigned to Duette Elementary to help handle
the burgeoning enrollment.)

Duette Elementary is an odd mixture of the old and the new.
Volunteers built the building in 1930 when Albritton, Bunker
Hill, and Duette schools were consolidated into one. The green
chalkboards and tongue-and-groove wooden interior walls definitely belong to an earlier day. For many years, Duette Elementary, which once taught students through the eighth grade,
was considered a "strawberry school" because there were no
classes during the strawberry picking season from January to
March.

Today, despite its remote location (it's 25 miles to the nearest
full-size elementary school), Duette Elementary is a technologi-
cal front-runner. Every student has his or her own computer,
compared to the average of one computer for every three students in other Manatee County schools.

While some teachers might be daunted by the prospect of
teaching grades kindergarten through five in one room at the
same time, Miss Donna enjoys the challenge, as is evidenced by
several Teacher of the Year nominations.

Because of its size and remoteness, it costs more to educate
Duette Elementary students than it does students at bigger
schools. But if School Board members had any thought of shut-
ting down the little school, local residents would urge them—
strongly—to think again. In fact, the local PTA—and Miss
Donna—are in favor of not only keeping but expanding the
school.

"We're on the cutting edge," says Miss Donna, who is doing
her Ph.D. thesis on the advantages of grade-integrated schools.

Duette Elementary School is located at the corner of State
Road 62 and Keenton Road, 18 miles east of US 301, in rural
eastern Manatee County. The phone number is (941) 721–6674.
The Web site is www.manatee.k12.fl.us.

TALES FROM THE CRYPT

*A*mong the diseases you least want to contract, yellow fever has to rank high on the list.

Symptoms of the mosquito-transmitted disease include chills, fever, headache, vomiting of blood, and bleeding from the gums and nose. The disease gets its name from the fact that some victims become jaundiced and turn yellow. When that happens, there's about a fifty-fifty chance you'll die.

Florida, with its warm climate and abundant lakes and ponds, is very popular with mosquitoes, which could explain why Florida has had so many yellow fever epidemics. The last big one in 1888 killed 400 people in Jacksonville and resulted in the long-overdue creation of the state Board of Health in 1889. By 1918, Florida was yellow fever–free.

Floridians don't think much about the disease now, but back in the early 1800's folks shivered with terror at the mere mention of the words yellow fever. It was a terrible disease and about the only good thing that came out of it was a colorful legend.

The story goes that yellow fever victims got so sick that they sometimes appeared dead before they really were. As a result, some victims were buried alive. This was apparently discovered when bodies were disinterred and moved to other cemeteries. Fingernail scratches were sometimes visible inside the coffin lid, and the padding inside was shredded. The "corpse" had obviously been trying to get out.

The solution to this problem involved some trial and error. First, they tried putting some pieces of fried chicken next to the corpse before closing the lid. This was OK in the sense that the victim could enjoy a nice picnic lunch when he woke up, but not OK in the sense that he was still 6 feet under ground with no way to get out. (Plus, they often forgot to pack potato salad.)

Next, they tried running an air tube into the coffins. This presumably allowed the victim to breathe, but still gave him no way out.

The final solution involved tying one end of a string to the victim's finger and the other end to a small bell aboveground. The idea was that if the dead person's finger twitched, the bell would ring, someone would hear it and summon help. The problem was that corpses tended to awake at inconvenient times, when people were away doing other things, like frying chicken or burying people alive. So people were hired to sit by fresh gravesites and listen for the tinkling of the bell. The work was divided into three shifts, the most unpopular being the midnight to 8:00 A.M. stint that came to be called the "graveyard shift."

Two other popular phrases were inspired by this morbid practice. Can you guess what they are?

Dead ringer and saved by the bell.

Or so the legend goes.

FLORIDA'S FIRST INCORPORATED BLACK TOWN
Eatonville

ora Neale Hurston, one of Florida's foremost authors, took pride in her home north of Orlando: "I was born in a Negro town. I do not mean by that the black back-side of an average town. Eatonville, Florida, is, and was at the time of my birth, a pure Negro town—charter, mayor, council, town marshal, and all. It was not the first Negro community in America, but it was the first to be incorporated, the first attempt at organized self-government on the part of Negroes in America."

Eatonville, founded in 1887, survives as a predominantly black community of about 2,000 people. Hurston, who was born in 1891 and died in 1960, is remembered in a namesake Museum of Fine Arts, along with an annual arts festival called Zora!

The Eatonville novelist went on to write *Jonah's Gourd Vine* and *Their Eyes Were Watching God,* along with an autobiography, *Dust Tracks on a Road.* Her books include hometown descriptions of the local general store and the "lying porch" where townspeople gathered.

Hurston's father, John, a minister and master carpenter, was an Alabama native drawn to Florida by the promise of a new settlement. The *Eatonville Speaker* newspaper offered notices such as this one on January 22, 1889: "Colored people of the United States—Solve the great race problem by securing a home in Eatonville, Florida, a Negro city governed by Negroes." Local accomplishments included the Hungerford School, modeled after the Tuskegee Institute, along with the Macedonia Missionary Baptist Church.

Both remain today, after a fashion, and both are part of a walking tour of the town sponsored by the Association to Preserve the Eatonville Community. What was the Old Apopka Road, and then Eatonville Road, is now Kennedy Boulevard. Plaques around town point out old pathways, cemeteries, and citrus groves.

For more information on Eatonville, call the town offices at (407) 623-1313. For more information on Historic Eatonville, call (407) 647-3307.

FREAKTOWN, USA
Gibsonton

Half a century ago, people who made their living as sideshow freaks wintered in a small town on the bay just south of Tampa. While walking to the post office or grocery store in Gibsonton, it wasn't unusual to run into a bearded lady, a three-legged man, or a human blockhead famous for hammering ice picks up his nose.

Sideshows are pretty much a thing of the past, but Gibsonton is still home to lots of circus and carnival folk. Many residents of this unpretentious town of 7,000 are ticket takers, clowns, acrobats, animal trainers, and ride mechanics.

The few remaining sideshow stars, who dubbed the place "Freaktown, USA," are reluctant to talk to reporters because of all the negative publicity brought down on Gibsonton by the Lobster Boy case.

Lobster Boy, a.k.a. Grady Stiles Jr., was born with a genetic condition that joined his fingers and toes into two-digit claws. He moved by flopping around on flipperlike legs. Needless to say, he was a sideshow celebrity. Unfortunately, Stiles was also a violent alcoholic. He was convicted of killing his daughter's boyfriend, but thanks to testimony from two of his neighbors—a fat man and a bearded lady—he was spared a lengthy prison term.

That's only the beginning of the story. Stiles was later murdered by his wife and stepson (a blockhead) who paid a hit man $1,500 to shoot him. Both are still serving time. Stiles's son by another marriage, who had the same affliction as his father, tried to make a name for himself in show business. He had a public access cable TV show in Tampa and tried selling tracings of his clawlike hand on eBay.

It was all very unpleasant and embarrassing stuff to the hard-working freaks (a hermaphrodite, an 8-foot-tall man, a woman who walks on glass) of Gibsonton who tried to make an honest living.

Sideshows were done in not so much by political correctness as by medical advances. Better treatments became available for people with physical abnormalities and pregnant women are now warned against taking certain drugs that can cause deformities.

The weather is still nice in the winter in Gibsonton, but you almost never see a bearded lady on your way to the post office anymore.

M o n k e y i n g   A r o u n d
H o m o s a s s a

As a tourist attraction, Monkey Island is not likely to put Disney World out of business anytime soon.

"It's just a bunch of monkeys on an island. What more do you need to know?" That's the way a gentleman at the bar at Charlie Brown's Crab House summed up the situation.

The story's not a great deal more complicated than that. A man by the name of Bruce Norris owned a wildlife attraction up the Homosassa River from the restaurant. When the state purchased the attraction, Norris took some of the ringtail monkeys and relocated them on a little spoil island in the middle of the river, a stone's throw from the restaurant. That was about sixty years ago, and the monkeys, or at least their descendants, remain.

There's a little red-and-white lighthouse on the island, some palm trees, and a tire swing on which the half dozen or so monkeys can cavort. (During our visit, there was precious little cavorting going on, though we did observe some serious languishing.)

Our barroom source told us the monkeys don't swim the few feet to shore because they've got it made on the island, what with daily feedings, the aforementioned tire swing, and a measure, albeit small, of local celebrity.

They were a semi-interesting diversion while we scarfed down a delicious soft-shell crab sandwich at Charlie Brown's, but we expect most folks who visit the river come to watch the manatees, not the monkeys.

After all, it's just a bunch of monkeys on an island. What more do you need to know?

Monkey Island is located right off the dock of Charlie Brown's Crab House in Homosassa Riverside Resort. Take County Road 490 west from Homosassa Springs to Homosassa and follow the signs. Phone (352) 628–2474.

MONUMENT TO THE KIDS
Kissimmee

A trickle of tourists still visit the Monument to the States, amazingly enough, which only proves the durability of even the most mundane tourist attractions. The Kissimmee monument, after all, is merely a tower of stones perched on a corner between the town's main drag and its lakefront park.

For locals, the monument is a relic of the past. During World War II a local booster named Charles Bressler-Pettis came up with the idea of collecting stones from all fifty states. For neighborhood kids, fifty years later, the monument is both a landmark and a dare.

The stone steps of the monument, you see, practically beg to be climbed. Easy handholds crowd all four sides, but there is a devilish overhang near the top of the 50-foot tower. A pair of local basketball players describe the Monument to the States as a Kissimmee rite of passage.

"Kids dare each other to climb to the top," says Michael Merritt, 15. "I made it like halfway and went back down."

Charles Ibbott, 13, points more than halfway up. "I got up to the Cape Cod part," he says. "I fell when I got to that red rock."

Considering that this rock is a good 30 feet off the ground, and the fact that Ibbott tells his story with a smile, this is a more dubious claim. Charles Bressler-Pettis, though, would appreciate his sense of promotion.

S P I C Y   A N D   " S P I C E Y "   B O I L E D   P E A N U T S
L a k e   H a m i l t o n

There's hardly a Panhandle highway, byway, or country lane that doesn't have some lonely soul selling boiled peanuts from a roadside stand. It's usually one person beside a pot filled with boiling nuts ready to be scooped out with a ladle that's sometimes made from a stick and a tin can punched with holes.

PEANUTS, the signs say, or P-NUTS. They're often hot peanuts and Cajun peanuts, or spicy and even "spicey" peanuts.

As tourists travel south into the Florida peninsula, boiled peanuts are fewer and farther in between. One of the last outposts is the Nut House, tucked between US 27 and Lake Hamilton west of Orlando and south of Interstate 4.

It's a "spicey" stop, brightly painted, offering quart bags of peanuts for $3.00 A Confederate flag hangs out back, and chickens cluck in a nearby orange grove as four lanes of traffic rumble by.

Amanda Flowers, a twenty-one-year-old Polk County native working the stand, said the Nut House has been a local favorite since before she was born. Now it's expanding its reach.

"We get people who come all the way here from Orlando and Miami," she said. "They come all the way here, get their peanuts, and turn around and go home. The lady who comes from Miami says there's a stand down there, but she likes ours better."

The Nut House offers green Virginia peanuts that have been soaked for forty-eight hours and boiled for four in a sixty-gallon pot. Regular peanuts are boiled with four cups of salt and a ham hock, while the spicy nuts also get Zatarain's crab boil and crushed red pepper.

Northern tourists often stop at the roadside stand to stretch their legs and satisfy their curiosity.

"They'll come by and never even heard of boiled peanuts," Flowers says. "We tell 'em about them and let 'em taste some."

The Nut House is just north of Lake Hamilton on the west side of US 27.

THE EERIE LEGEND OF SPOOK HILL
Lake Wales

Once upon a time, at a place not far from what is now a convenience store, an Indian town on Lake Wales was plagued by a huge alligator. The town's great warrior chief and the gator were killed in a titanic struggle that created the huge, swampy depression nearby. The chief was buried on the north side of the depression.

Later, pioneer haulers coming from the old Army trail atop the ridge found their horses laboring here, at the foot of the ridge, and called the place Spook Hill.

Is it the gator seeking revenge, or is the chief protecting his land?

Does any of this make any sense to you?

It doesn't make any difference, because the fun of Spook Hill is sitting in your car as it rolls . . . uphill. Or at least that's the way it seems. A sign near the bottom of the hill on North Wales Drive instructs you to stop on the white line and put your car in neutral. Your eyes tell you you're headed downhill, but your car tells you otherwise.

Be sure to check your rearview mirror for cars behind you before you investigate the optical illusion that is Spook Hill; not only do you roll backward, you do so briskly.

Spook Hill is located just down the hill from the intersection of North Wales Drive and Burns Avenue. Small brown signs scattered about town direct you to the place. Right around the corner is Spook Hill Elementary School, the logo for which is, appropriately enough, a ghost. Mind your speed when driving by the school in the morning and afternoon. The tickets the cops hand out are no optical illusion.

Mountain Music
Lake Wales

You won't need Sherpa guides or bottled oxygen to scale the highest "peak" in peninsular Florida.

Located in Lake Wales in Polk County, Iron Mountain tops out at a decidedly nondizzying height of 298 feet above sea level. In other words, it's not quite as high as a football field is long. Forget mountain goats and glaciers; the view from the top is mostly of nondescript orange groves.

Bok's Singing Tower in Lake Wales is one of the most restful places in Central Florida. Just watch out for the squirrels.

In fact, Iron Mountain wouldn't be worthy of mention at all if weren't for Bok's Singing Tower rising from what can laughingly be called its summit. Opened to the public on February 1, 1929, by President Calvin Coolidge, Bok Tower is a 205-foot-high bell tower that houses sixty bronze carillon bells ranging in weight from sixteen pounds to nearly twelve tons. Clock music is played by a mechanical keyboard every half hour beginning at 10:00 A.M. A lengthier recital chimes at 3:00 P.M.

The tower, a gift to the American people from Dutch publisher and author Edward W. Bok, is constructed of pink and gray marble from Georgia and coquina stone (a sort of concrete made with seashells) from St. Augustine. The tower's sculpture and tile work, called faience, depict mostly birds and plants as well as other varieties of wildlife, including seahorses, fish, foxes, tortoises, and, oddly enough, apes.

Surrounded by a moat, the tower is the centerpiece of Bok Tower Gardens, 200 acres of immaculately maintained azaleas, camellias, magnolias, and other flowering tees and plants. A colony of brightly colored wood ducks makes its home in the gardens, as do more than one hundred other wild bird species. The birds are indeed abundant, but the first thing you will notice is the squirrels, which scamper about everywhere and are not the least bit shy about begging a handout.

The tower, more a work of art than a monument (visitors aren't allowed inside), is a National Historic Landmark, and the gardens are a designated site on the Great Florida Birding Trail. The place is all about beauty and serenity; you'd have to be an uptight person indeed not to feel your cares melt away after spending an hour or two wandering the grounds.

Bok, a Dutch immigrant following the advice of his grandmother, said he wanted to make America more beautiful because he lived in it. Bok Tower Gardens is proof of his success.

Bok Tower Gardens, located at 1151 Tower Boulevard, Lake Wales, is open every day of the year from 8:00 A.M. to 6:00 P.M. Admission is $6.00 for adults, $2.00 for children five through twelve, and free for children under five. All visitors are admitted free on Saturday before 9:00 A.M.

ESTATE LIVING

*W*hile visiting Bok Tower Gardens, don't forget to tour Pinewood Estate, a twenty-room Mediterranean Revival–style villa on eight acres next to the gardens. Pinewood was called "El Retiro" when it opened in 1929 and was the winter home of C. Austin Buck (not Bok), vice president of Bethlehem Steel. Buck's love of Latin lifestyle and architecture is reflected by his use of Cuban tiles throughout the house and a Spanish frog fountain leading to a grotto in front. Buck hired Frederick Law Olmsted Jr. to design the gardens in keeping with the ecology of Florida. Today, the Pine Ridge Nature Trail, Woodland Garden, and Wildlife Observatory are testimony to that commitment.

Guided tours of Pinewood Estate are offered daily from October through mid-May, at 11:00 A.M. and 1:30 P.M. A six-week special event called Christmas at Pinewood takes place each year beginning the day after Thanksgiving.

Phone (863) 676–1408 or visit www.boktower.org.

To get there, take exit 23 from Interstate 4 and drive south on US 27 for about 20 miles. Go past Eagle Ridge Mall for two traffic lights, then turn left on Mountain Lake Cutoff Road and follow the signs. From Tampa and Vero Beach, take State Road 60 to Lake Wales and follow the signs.

SPACE COAST COUNTDOWN
Melbourne

In 1998, when it was time for a new telephone area code in central Florida, a man named Robert "Ozzie" Osband had a singular idea. The Titusville programmer and consultant—he calls himself a "computerist"—thought he had the perfect new area code for Brevard County, Cape Canaveral, and what's known as "The Space Coast."

3-2-1.

Get it? 3-2-1, as in blast off.

Osband's idea for the area code was an immediate hit. Governor Jeb Bush called it "a brilliant idea" at a National Space Club dinner, and the number was adopted by the Florida Public Service Commission. In 1999, the change even appeared as a final question on Jeopardy: "In 1999, several counties around Cape Canaveral, Florida, were assigned this new telephone area code." The correct answer, of course, was "What is 3-2-1?"

On his Spacey Ideas Web site, Osband crowed that "321 is MY area code! (But I share.) I asked for it, they approved, so it's mine, right?" He also published *Via Oz,* a fanzine explaining the development of the area code. At a computer conference, under the hacker identity of "The Cheshire Catalyst," he gave a talk called "How I Got My Own Area Code."

Last, but not least, or at least for a brief while, Osband snagged the coolest phone number in the area: (321) LIFTOFF.

ROCK OF AGES
Mulberry

The Mulberry Phosphate Museum may well be the world's only museum dedicated to . . . fertilizer.

The galleries, some of which are inside a train caboose, tell the story of phosphate, a gray rock mined extensively in and around Mulberry in a section of the state known as Bone Valley. The name comes from the fact that the phosphate rock, formed millions of years ago when Florida was under water, is intermingled with Cenozoic era fossils. The fossilized bones of mastodons, saber-toothed tigers, rhinos, and boxcar-length prehistoric sharks are on display in another part of the little museum.

The Phosphate Museum in Mulberry may be the world's only museum devoted to fertilizer.

The phosphate rock is gouged out of the ground with giant draglines, the buckets on which are the size of a small house and can remove 70,000 pounds of material in a single scoop. The museum has a dragline bucket on the grounds. You can stand inside it and have your picture taken. Drive less than a mile east of town on State Road 60 and you can see for yourself what phosphate mining does to the countryside. (Think moonscape.)

The self-guided museum tour briefly addresses the problems associated with phosphate mining, which include water pollution and habitat destruction, but because the museum is by, for, and of the phosphate industry, the displays mostly concentrate on the positive aspects of phosphate.

Indeed, phosphate is an important ingredient in fertilizer and animal feed. Many household items contain phosphate, or a derivative of phosphate, including Crest toothpaste, Purina Puppy Chow, and Slim-Fast. And that tingle you get when you take a swig of Coca-Cola? Phosphoric acid. (And all this time you thought it was a sugar high.)

The fact that you might be brushing your teeth with ten-million-year-old crab poop could be disconcerting to some, which is why the phosphate industry would rather you think of the stuff in terms of bountiful harvests and an answer to world hunger.

(Also, it is not true that the phosphate museum's video presentation lasts ten million years. It just seems that long.)

The Mulberry Phosphate Museum is located at 101 S.E. First Street, at the corner of State Road 37 in Mulberry. The museum is open Tuesday through Saturday from 10:00 A.M. to 4:30 P.M. Admission is free, but donations are accepted. Phone (863) 425–2823.

GRAPE EXPECTATIONS
Myakka City

Nestled amid the orange groves, cattle ranches, and tomato fields of eastern Manatee County, the Rosa Fiorelli Winery is about as far from Napa Valley as you can get, both geographically and psychologically.

The fact that wine is made at all in Florida is an oddity; the fact that the Fiorelli wines taste pretty darned good is nothing short of astonishing. Natives of Sicily, Antonio Fiorelli and his wife, Rosa, have been growing muscadine and blanc du bois wine grapes in these parts for almost fifteen years, confounding the conventional wisdom that central Florida's heat, humidity, and sandy soil would make such a thing impossible.

Although it's unlikely that Florida wines will ever cause the Mondavi family to lose any sleep, the industry is slowly growing. The Fiorellis produced about 8,000 cases of red and white wines in 2000, with individual bottles selling for $10 to $15. Antonio proclaims Manatee Red, a union of Florida and California grapes, to be his best wine to date. His 1998 Manatee Red won the silver medal in the International Wine Competition at the 2001 Florida State Fair. (He's shooting for the gold next time.)

The grapes are harvested from the ten-acre vineyard in June; the wine making takes place in a garage-size building on the grounds. In Florida, as it is everywhere, wine making is a lot of work.

"You've got to constantly check the grapes for insects, mold, mildew, everything," says Antonio. "If you think all there is to it is sticking a grapevine in the ground and walking away, you won't make it."

With some award-winning wines to his credit and public awareness of this most unusual of Florida crops increasing, Antonio Fiorelli figures to be one of the ones who will make it. The fact that he named his winery after his wife didn't hurt either.

The Rosa Fiorelli Winery is located at 4020 County Road 675. For tasting information, call (914) 322–0976.

Somewhere, Over the Swampy Bog
On a

From the swamps of Hardee County rises Solomon's Castle, one man's rural image of Oz. Naturally, there's a yellow brick road leading up to the place, which belongs to Howard Solomon, part tinkerer, part artist, and 100 percent a hoot.

Variously called the Da Vinci of Debris or Rembrandt of Reclamation, Solomon has created a 12,000-square-foot museum/home/castle/restaurant/gallery that invariably leaves visitors scratching their heads. The "shingles" of the castle are aluminum offset printing plates discarded by the *Herald-Advocate* newspaper in nearby Wauchula. The turrets sparkle with stained-glass windows made by Solomon, and at the entrance are two armored statues, one white, the other black, called Day and Knight.

Funny wordplay, you will quickly discover, is as big a part of the Solomon's Castle experience as the 200 pieces of "found art." Solomon does not just conduct a tour; he gives a performance. He steers visitors past an animal menagerie made of fifty pounds of coat hangers, then on to a motorcycle made from an old corn planter, nicknamed "Evil Corn-Evil." Keep your eye open for the goblin under the living room floor and the kitchen elevator that runs on a car battery.

All of the art is made from junk either found by Solomon or donated to him. There are cars and chairs made of beer cans, a lion made of five oil drums cut into pieces, and a gun collection that would probably not meet with the approval of Charlton Heston. One gun, made of half a hacksaw and a jack, is called "Hacked-Off Jacksaw." Alongside is a pair of dueling pistols with their barrels bent backward. Solomon claims, with a straight face, that they belonged to the Rev. Jim Jones.

A high-school dropout, Solomon became proficient in more than twenty trades, including welding, shipbuilding, carpentry, and plumbing. While other more conventional artists might have paint and brushes in their studios, Solomon's is filled with welders, steel saws, wood saws, grinders, sandblasters, and shears. Some of the machines Solomon made himself as a teenager.

A native of Rochester, New York, Solomon moved to Florida when he was twenty-one. He bought fifty-five acres of land in rural Hardee County, not knowing that the property became a swamp in the summer. But that wasn't much of a problem for the resourceful Solomon. He built levees and installed pumps to drain the land. Perhaps to remind himself of his mistake, Solomon dug a moat around his castle and built the Boat on the Moat restaurant, fashioned after a Spanish galleon.

Solomon's Castle is open for lunch from 11:00 A.M. to 4:00 P.M. Tuesday through Sunday, and for dinner on Saturday from 6:00 to 11:00 P.M. The castle is closed in September. Admission is $7.50 for adults, $3.00 for children. For information, call (863) 494–6077.

From Bradenton, drive east on State Road 64 28 miles past the Interstate 75 overpass. Turn right on County Road 665 and drive 9 more miles. Solomon Road will be on your left.

WORLD'S LARGEST MCDONALD'S
Orlando

Orlando wouldn't be Orlando—a mind-boggling expanse of tourism great and small, bright and loud, tacky and tackier—without the World's Largest McDonald's and PlayPlace. If Mickey D's wasn't there, to paraphrase Voltaire's famous quip about God, it would have been necessary to invent it.

It fits Orlando like the ears on that other Mickey's head.

This McDonald's claims to be the largest, but so do a few others. This McDonald's is busy, located between Interstate 4 and International Drive, but franchises in Moscow and Beijing have more customers. No, it's not size or scale that makes this "the most unique McDonald's in the world." In a fast-food chain that prizes conformity above all else—a french fry in Tampa must taste exactly like a french fry in Tacoma—this Mickey D's is downright strange, even by Orlando standards.

Along with the three-story jungle gym and video game arcade, there is a pizza counter and ice-cream parlor (both closed on a recent visit). There is a small alligator tank, courtesy of Gatorland (empty on a recent visit). There is a waterfall, plus a souvenir stand and a birthday party area with a throne set next to a Ronald McDonald statue.

A page one *Orlando Sentinel* story from August 16, 1992, is framed on the wall. The headline: "McEverything but the McKitchen Sink."

In the Maui room, decorated with a Hawaiian motif, a small plaque hidden behind a garbarge can explains the personality behind the place. It seems that owners Gary and Jeanie Oerther were married on the island, and it's their favorite place in the world—after Orlando. The golden-arched signs in the parking lot, instead of saying WELCOME, offer ALOHA.

Besides all the food and entertainment, the place offers life lessons, including "Ronald's Way to Play":

1. Be a friend! Take turns and share. Big kids, help the little kids and have fun!

2. Leave toys, food, and other stuff back at the tables.

3. Play safe! Enter the play area slowly, so you don't bump into anybody.

4. Leave your shoes here!

5. Kids 3 to 12 can play. Parents, too!

Those parents may or may not enjoy Mickey D's, but kids take to the place the way fries take to ketchup. They're scarfing down food, clambering through the jungle gym, and pouring tokens into the video games.

For many, it looks like a visit to Orlando wouldn't be a visit to Orlando without a stop at the World's Largest McDonald's.

Mickey D's is at 6875 Sandlake Road, exit 29 off I–4. Call (407) 351–2185 for more information.

WORLD'S LARGEST STRAWBERRY
Plant City

OK, it's not really a strawberry; it's just a painting of one, atop the water tower in Plant City. But if there were an official world's largest strawberry, you'd probably find it here, in the self-described "Winter Strawberry Capital of the World."

Plant City, in eastern Hillsborough County, is to strawberries what Indian River is to oranges and Apalachicola is to oysters. Twenty percent of America's strawberries come from Florida, and a good portion of those are grown in Hillsborough County. When most people think of Hillsborough County, they think of the big city of Tampa. Few know that Hillsborough has 2,600 fruit and vegetable farms, an annual agricultural output worth $400 million.

Plant City hosts an annual strawberry festival that dates back to 1930. Held in late February and early March, the festival features a strawberry shortcake eating contest, a strawberry picking contest, and, of course, the crowning of Miss Strawberry. (Shannon Davis Hinson was the 2002 winner.) While some may come for the swine and steer judging, most come to gorge on strawberries, with or without shortcake.

Quick strawberry trivia question: How do you know that you have no life? Answer: When your idea of a good time is counting the number of seeds on a strawberry. We'll save you the trouble; the average number is 200.

Plant City is not, as you might expect, named after the pervasive strawberry plant. It's named after Henry Plant, a bigshot Florida railroad tycoon who fixed the little town up with its first set of tracks back in 1885. The town was called Hichipuckassa at the time, but citizens wisely decided to rename the town after its benefactor.

A Hichipuckassa Strawberry Festival just wouldn't have the same ring to it.

DQU, AND THE U IS FOR URINAL
Port Charlotte

Turn off Interstate 75 at exit 31, stop at the Texaco gas station with a Subway and Dairy Queen, and look at the front window of the DQ. Beside the usual ads for "The Original Blizzard," you'll find a flyer taped to the door.

VOTED ONE OF THE TOP 5 MOST FASCINATING URINALS IN THE WORLD!

Joining the ranks of the facilities at the New York Marathon, London's Millennium Dome, the public rest room at Rothesay in Scotland, and the Kowloon Sheraton Hotel in Hong Kong is the women's urinal here in Port Charlotte

It might make you lose your appetite, but it will certainly pique your curiosity. If you ask the DQ clerks what the heck the sign means, they'll sigh and point to the ladies' rest room. Go to that rest room, knock loudly to make sure no one is inside, and you'll get your first glimpse of what the French might call *un pissoir pour les femmes.*

Yes, indeed, it's a urinal for women. A "she-inal," if you will, that allows women to urinate while standing up. It is perhaps one of a kind, and that's the reason it attracted the interest of a certain Internet Web site that ranked it fourth among the world's urinals.

Besides gaining recognition on Urinal.net, the "she-inal" has gotten attention from local newspapers and far-off radio stations. Journalists contact store owner Jim Coulter, who welcomes the attention. The "she-inal" was developed about ten years ago by a Pensacola woman named Kathie Jones. It was marketed by a company called Urinette, which is no longer in business. Coulter believes a previous owner installed the device in an attempt to get around adding facilities for the handicapped.

At least a few customers, after learning about the rest room on-line, have made a point of visiting the Dairy Queen on trips to southwest Florida. Becky Bovell, Charlotte County tourism director, told the Charlotte *Herald-Tribune* that any publicity is good publicity. "If it brings even one person to Charlotte County, that's a good thing," she said. "I'm sure we will be flushed with excitement."

TRACKING AN EIGHT-TRACK TAPE COLLECTOR
Port Charlotte

Once upon a time, before Madonna and MTV, before compact discs and MP3s, there was a commercial recording format known as eight-track tape. The big, clunky tapes came along in the late 1960s and allowed people to listen to their favorite music in their cars. At the time, this was a very big deal. Soon, of course, there were audiocassettes, and then digital music formats, and eight-track went the way of the dodo bird.

Except, of course, for "trackers" such as Stephen Pearl, 54, of Port Charlotte.

He prefers the hiss and hum of old tapes to the cold quiet of the most modern technology. From a workshop in his small apartment, he collects eight-track tapes—pre-Beatles rock and roll, mostly—and repairs eight-track players.

"It's good therapy for me, and I hate to see people throw eight-tracks away when they're still good," Pearl says. "I don't charge people hardly anything because I'm not really doing it for the money."

For eight-track fans, there's a whole subculture devoted to the medium. A Web site, 8-Track Heaven, promises to be "digi-

"Tracker" Stephen Pearl of Port Charlotte stands before his collection of eight-track tapes. Eight-tracks are making a comeback among collectors who like tape untangling as much as they like music.

tal online, but analog at heart." A documentary, *So Right They're Wrong,* followed fans underground, where they read a quarterly magazine, *8-Track Mind,* and follow Eight Noble Truths.

These include "Naive is not a dirty word," "New and improved don't necessarily mean the same thing," and "State of the art is in the eye of the beholder."

Pearl might be proof of that. He's got CD players and everything else, but enjoys an afternoon spent cracking open plastic boxes and splicing tape. He's disabled, a former security guard with bifocals and a graying beard, and has plenty of time to devote to his hobby.

"When you go to digital, I think you lose a lot," he says. "Everything's perfect, and the original recordings were never perfect. Personally, I don't think anything modern sounds as good."

A NINETY-ONE-YEAR-OLD SNAKE CHARMER
Punta Gorda

Even at the age of ninety-one, closing in on an astonishing century of risk and adventure, Bill Haast still tangles with cobras. Every morning the Punta Gorda man collects venom from hissing and lunging cobras, along with vipers, rattlesnakes, and coral snakes. He pulls them from cages, coming within inches of their fangs before seizing them behind the head with swift, sure hands.

The New Jersey native, a flight engineer during World War II, still injects himself with venom every other day. The idea is to build up his immunity in case accidental bites from poisonous snakes. He's survived some 169 bites, a mark recognized by the *Guinness Book of World Records,* so he must be doing something right.

Medical researchers still use Haast's freeze-dried venom, but he made his fame and fortune with an old Florida tourist attraction called the Miami Serpentarium. Even today, when safer methods are available, he's happy to demonstrate snake-handling skills for the film crews who make pilgrimages to his Gulf Coast laboratory.

For the last twelve years, Bill and Nancy Haast have lived and worked along Shell Creek in eastern Charlotte County. She's his fifty-five-year-old wife, lab assistant, press liaison,

You're over ninety, you're living in paradise, you're . . . handling snakes?!? Ninety-one-year-old Bill Haast from Punta Gorda is a living legend among Florida snake handlers.

office manager, and friendly voice on the phone. They're busy every day, caring for the laboratory, grounds, and more than 1,000 poisonous snakes.

"You know, our lives, we're pretty focused," Nancy says, laughing. "We're not like most people."

For many snake handlers in Florida, Haast is a still-living legend. Bruce Dangerfield, a Vero Beach animal control officer, helps supply Haast with poisonous snakes, bringing along friends to visit the spry old man in Punta Gorda. "He's my hero, without a doubt," Dangerfield says. "It's just amazing to see the things he does. He's bouncing around like a kid, and he's sharp as a tack. I'll tell you what, he's the most fantastic person I've ever met."

Critics call Haast an exhibitionist, someone who takes needless risks, but Dangerfield finds that part of the old man's charm. "He's probably a little safer when he's by himself; I'm sure Nancy sees to that," he says. "He's still a showman—not a showoff, but a showman."

Just about every day, Haast wears white—white shirt, white belt, white pants—a practice that dates back to his shows at the Serpentarium. He's got a shock of white hair that Nancy trims for him, because he won't bother going to town for a haircut. When *Outside* magazine did an interview with him in 1996, the photo was dramatically lit, making Haast look like the mad scientist in an old black-and-white movie.

In person, though, Haast has an easy laugh and strong memory for names, dates, and places. He's short and trim, about as fit as a ninety-one-year-old man can be. Except for his hands: They're still quick enough to catch cobras, but his fingers are crabbed and swollen from the bites he's gotten over the years. He's missing his right pinkie from a cottonmouth bite. The latest bite came from a rattlesnake last year, but Haast shrugged it off. His hand was swollen for just a few days.

Both Haasts would like their venom collection business to continue after they're gone. Nancy has a list of apprentices who could help with the snake handling if something happened to Bill. Haast remains healthy enough to laugh at the idea.

"If I go before Nancy, we've got no problem," he says, flashing a big smile. "If she goes before me, then we've got a problem. I can't even work the computer." The Haast laboratory is not open to the public, but there are occasional group tours. For more information, call (941) 639–8888.

TOURIST ATTRACTIONS, B.D. (BEFORE DISNEY)
Sarasota

If it's long lines, high prices, and stomach-churning roller coasters you're looking for, than Sarasota Jungle Gardens is not the place for you.

One of Florida's oldest tourist attractions, Jungle Gardens was a swampy banana grove in the early 1930s when Sarasota newspaperman David Lindsay bought the ten-acre tract with the idea of turning the virgin subtropical jungle into a botanical garden.

Lindsay and his partner, Pearson Conrad, brought in thousands of tropical plants, trees, and flowers from all over the world. Artesian well–fed streams and a central lake give the place the feel of a leafy oasis just a few blocks from busy US 41.

Opened in December 1940 as a tourist attraction, Sarasota Jungle Gardens has changed little over the years, which adds

Forget roller coasters and fireworks; flamingos are the centerpiece of Sarasota's Jungle Gardens, one of Florida's oldest tourist attractions.

considerably to its unique charm. As you begin walking the trail beneath a canopy of Australian nut trees, bunya-bunya trees, strangler figs, and royal palms, you feel as if you are alone in the place. Abundant benches encourage the visitor to pause and enjoy the tranquility, or maybe engage the resident kookaburra or spider monkey in conversation.

Probably the favorite place to pause in Jungle Gardens is Flamingo Lagoon, where black swans, white swans, and, of course, flamingos make you wish you had brought along more color film. (The good folks in the gift shop will be happy to fix you up.)

But even a low-key tourist attraction needs a spectacle of
some sort, and at Jungle Gardens, the *Birds of the Rainforest*
show is unquestionably the main event. Have you ever seen a
bird roller skate, balance atop a basketball, or ride a bicycle on
a high wire? Trained macaws and cockatoos do these things
and more.

Frosty, a greater sulfur-crested cockatoo, is sixty-six years
old and has been doing his act at Jungle Gardens since 1972.
Frosty appeared on the *Ed Sullivan Show;* others, like Paulette,
a blue and gold macaw, have starred in commercials.

Believe it or not, the birds were trained by inmates at Chino
State Prison in California as part of a prisoner enrichment pro-
gram designed to teach sensitivity and respect. (If the birds
learned any rough language while in prison, they have the
good manners to keep it to themselves.)

Don't forget to visit the reptile exhibit, which contains live
specimens of every American poisonous snake except the coral
snake, which does not fare well in captivity. The main attraction here is a 14-foot African rock python that was found slith-
ering about in the woods about 10 miles east of Jungle Gardens
near Interstate 75. The 200-pound snake was apparently somebody's pet that escaped.

No word yet on whether the prisoners at Chino have any interest in teaching this fella how to ride a bicycle on a high wire.

Sarasota Jungle Gardens, located at 3701 Bay Shore Road, is
open every day except Christmas from 9:00 A.M. to 5:00 P.M.
Daily admission prices range from $6.00 to $9.00; annual
passes are available. For more information, call (941) 355–5305
or visit the Web site www.sarasotajunglegardens.com.

TAC THE KNIFE
Sarasota

Meet Tom Johanning, maker of the TAC-11, the knife preferred by Rambos the world over.

Johanning is a machinist and owner of the prosaically named Florida Knife Company. You've probably never heard of him unless you're a Navy SEAL, a SEAL wanna-be, or the kind of person who wants a knife that can hack off a tree limb or pry open a car door and still remain sharp enough to shave the hairs off your arm.

The TAC in the name is short for "tactical" and the 11 means it's 11 inches long. This is not the kind of knife you whittle sticks with while rocking on the front porch.

Only you can tell you why you need a TAC-11, but we can tell you how it's made. Start with a bar of A-8 high-grade tool steel, machine shape it to specifications within two-thousandths of an inch, and then hand grind it into its final shape. Next, heat treat it at 1,700 degrees Fahrenheit before tempering it and cold treating it at 100 degrees below zero. Then add a grip and finish it by hand.

With the one-piece design, the thickness of the steel, and all of the hardening methods, this might be the strongest knife in the world. The knives cost $375 each, which could explain why there are only about 200 out there.

Although the fifty-nine-year-old machinist is proud of his work, you're not likely to see one of his creations hanging from his belt.

"I'm not really a knife guy," says the knife guy, pausing at how odd this sounds.

"Well, I make them, and I collect them, but I'm not the kind of guy who kayaks or climbs mountains or jumps out of airplanes."

When he has time, boating is what Johanning likes to do. Does he keep a couple of TAC-11s on hand in case he's attacked by kayak-paddling terrorists or a giant squid? Not hardly. The only blade he carries is a little bitsy pocketknife.

"Ninety percent of the time I use it to open boxes," said the knife man, smiling.

Florida Knife Company is located at 1735 Apex Road in Sarasota. Phone (941) 371–2104.

HELLO, DALI
St. Petersburg

There is absolutely no reason why there should be a Salvador Dali museum in downtown St. Petersburg, unless the city's brutal summer heat is somehow suggestive of melting clocks. And yet there it sits, on Third Street South, overlooking Bayboro Harbor, in the city better known for its green park benches and its reputation as Wrinkle City or God's Waiting Room. Dali, the flamboyant surrealist who loved to tease and surprise his audiences, must be laughing in his grave.

The story of how the Dali Museum came to St. Petersburg begins in, of all places, Cleveland. Industrialist A. Reynolds Morse and Eleanor Reese saw Dali's works for the first time in 1942 when a New York Museum of Modern Art traveling exhibition came to town. The couple, who were soon to be married, were immediately smitten by Dali's dreamlike imagery, perhaps best represented by the soft timepieces of the surrealist's most famous work, *The Persistence of Memory.*

After their marriage, the Morses began a correspondence with Dali and his Russian-born wife, Gala, developing a close friendship that lasted four decades. By the early 1970s, the Morses had assembled the largest private collection of Dali art in the world. From 1971 to 1980, they exhibited their collection in a wing of their office building in Beechwood, Ohio, near Cleveland. But the collection eventually grew too large for its quarters, and in the late '70s the Morses began searching for a permanent home for the works. There was one catch: Whoever accepted the collection had to agree to keep all the artwork and its massive amounts of descriptive material intact.

Enter St. Petersburg attorney James W. Martin. Martin read a *Wall Street Journal* article about how the art world had left the Dali collection in limbo. When he found out the Morses wanted to donate their collection to a tourist-oriented community in order to give more exposure to the works, Martin organized a group of local movers and shakers, forming the Dali Task Force. City and state funding was quickly secured, and the rest, as they say, is history.

The $2 million gallery occupies what was once a marine storage warehouse overlooking scenic Bayboro Harbor. The Morses personally selected the site because it reminded them of Cadaques, the Spanish town on the Mediterranean Sea where Dali grew up and began to paint.

Since opening in 1982, the museum has attracted thousands of visitors from around the world. In fact, six out of ten visitors come from outside the United States. What they come to see are ninety-five original oil paintings, more than one hundred watercolors and drawings and nearly thirteen hundred graphics, sculptures, objets d'art, photos, and descriptive materials.

The museum traces the curve of Dali's career from 1914 (when he was ten years old) to 1980. The artist died in Spain in 1989.

Although Dali was skilled in classical and other styles of art, it is his work in the form known as surrealism for which he is best remembered. Surrealism was founded in Paris in 1924 by André Breton. The surrealists believed that logic had failed humanity, so they turned to the unconscious and dreams as a way of explaining existence. Heavily influenced by the writings of Sigmund Freud, Dali used symbolic images such as crucifixes and the statue *Venus de Milo* to explore his own fears and fantasies. (Fortunately for fans of his art, Dali had plenty of these to work with.) He referred to these paintings as "hand-painted dream photographs."

Dali's flamboyant style and enormous ego did not sit well with other surrealists who attempted to expel him from the group at a "trial" held in Paris in 1934. The artist responded to the charges in a way that was quintessentially Dali: "The difference between me and the surrealists," he said, "is that I *am* Surrealism."

You can view the works of the man who was Surrealism Monday through Saturday from 9:30 A.M. to 5:30 P.M., until 8 P.M. on Thursday, and on Sunday from noon to 5:30 P.M. The museum is closed on Thanksgiving Day and Christmas.

General admission is $10.00, $7.00 for senior citizens sixty-five and older, and $5.00 for students. Children under ten are admitted free. On Thursdays, admission is half price after 5:00 P.M. The Salvador Dali Museum is located at 1000 Third Street South, St. Petersburg. For more information, phone (813) 823–3767 or go to the Web site www.daliweb.com or www.salvadordalimuseum.org.

STILL SHUFFLING ALONG
St. Petersburg

The St. Petersburg Shuffleboard Club, the oldest in Florida, was once the largest too. In its heyday after World War II, the club had 4,000 members and dozens of courts, including a grandstand arena with lights for evening play and stadium seating for 400 spectators. These days, though, the facility is showing its age, and there are only 188 members, leaving the courts empty much of the time.

What happened?

"Well, the world changed," says Mary Eldridge, the club president. "We may get the place about half full for tournaments. Now traffic is so hideous, people want to get out as soon as they're done playing. Years ago, people would stay until the last shot."

The shuffleboard club still offers sixty-five courts beside Mirror Lake in central St. Petersburg. The fixtures may be old, with peeling paint here and there, but the playing surfaces are level best.

"We make sure we have the best equipment," says Eldridge. "If you can't play here, you can't play anywhere. If you *can* play here, it's a nice place to play."

St. Pete tour buses pass by and offer the shuffleboard courts as a place of historical interest. The club lost a bit of its history, though, when the World Shuffleboard Hall of Fame was relocated to Clearwater. Eldridge has an explanation for that too.

"Well, politics," she says. "We're still trying to devise ways to get it back."

The shuffleboard club is located at 559 Mirror Lake Drive. It's open to the public during daylight hours when there are no leagues or tournament play. For more information, call (727) 822-2083.

LET'S GET CRACKING
Sebring

It's not as easy being a Florida cracker as it used to be.

In the old days, before semis and interstate highways, you just rounded up your cattle on horseback and herded them along to your destination. You didn't need a permit from anybody, and an obstacle as modest as a fence was considered a newfangled nuisance.

Today, members of the Florida Cracker Trail Association try to emulate the rustic, nomadic life that Florida crackers knew a century ago. In early March, for the past fifteen years, more than one hundred cowboys (and cowgirls) saddle up and ride across the state, on or near the old cattle drive trail that connects Manatee County on the west coast to Fort Pierce on the east.

The trip requires quite a bit of planning. The group needs a sheriff's escort as it plods 15 to 20 miles a day along the shoulders of state roads and U.S. highways. All horses must have updated veterinary records, the crackers need to find landowners who will let the group camp on their pastures, and a catering service must be hired to stay ahead of the group and prepare all their meals.

Rolling along behind the procession is a water tank, portable toilets, and trailers for any injured horses. To the riders' credit, no satellite dishes or microwave ovens were observed.

About halfway across the state, the riders stop in Sebring at, appropriately enough, Cracker Trail Elementary School. The kids get to pet the horses, and the crackers pop their whips for them (hence the name) and tell them stories of cracker life in old Florida, some of which may even be true.

The most authentic part of the whole trip may be the grub: breakfasts of biscuits and gravy and dinners of roasted chicken, swamp cabbage, and sweet tea. Then the campfire is lit and the serious business of swapping tall tales begins.

In the old days, the long ride would have been about herding and selling livestock. Today, people do it for different reasons, like fellowship and keeping history alive.

Roger Haney of Wauchula, the Florida Cracker Trail Association's founder and organizer of its first ride, takes a simpler view.

"We just did it for the heck of it," he said.

Florida Cracker Trail Association, Inc., 5310 19th Avenue, West Bradenton 34209. Carol Felts is the ride secretary. Phone (941) 798–3532; online at www.crackertrail.org/.

A BAR THAT DOESN'T SERVE DRINKS
Stuart

The southeast coast of Florida looked a lot different in the late 1800s than it does today. Condominiums, resorts, and luxury homes now stretch in an almost uninterrupted line from Fort Pierce to Key Biscayne. Millions of people are crammed into a narrow aisle of land bordered on the west by the Everglades and the east by the Atlantic Ocean.

But in the 1870s, in that same part of the state, there was pretty much . . . nothing. A newspaper writer of the day described the southeast coast as "unpopulated," adding that anyone unfortunate enough to wash up on its shores was likely to die of starvation or thirst, assuming he or she wasn't killed by a panther or bear first.

The U.S. Lifesaving Service, an arm of the U.S. Treasury, was aware of the problem. To provide aid to stranded sea travelers, it improved upon the idea of Bernie Pinsky, a Massachusetts man who in 1787 began building a series of 6-by-8-foot huts along that state's rocky coast to provide temporary shelter for shipwreck survivors.

There were several problems with Pinsky's huts. For starters, thieves kept stealing the blankets, coffee, cots, and first-aid kits stored there. If a shipwreck victim did manage to stumble upon one of the shelters, which was unlikely given the size of the hut and the unevenness of the coast, he was scarcely better off than he was before. Finally, because the huts were unmanned and infrequently monitored, there was a good chance the survivor would not be discovered for a long time.

The Lifesaving Service decided a better way to go was to build a set of ten manned life stations, spacing them out at

*If you were a shipwreck survivor who washed up on Hutchinson
Island near Stuart in the late 1800s, Gilbert's Bar House of
Refuge would have been a welcome sight indeed.*

approximately 26-mile intervals along the coast. The keeper of each home lived there full time. His job was to patrol the beach regularly (on foot, of course) between the station to the north and the station to the south, a round trip that took about three days. He carried a rope with him to pull ashore victims stranded beyond the breakers. It was exceptionally lonely, boring work, and few keepers stayed on more than a year. Survivors stayed in the attics of the houses, which were furnished like dormitories. Most survivors hitched a ride on a passing ship within two weeks.

Gilbert's Bar House of Refuge, built in 1876, is the last standing Florida house of refuge. A display there gives a terse account of those rare days when the keeper of the house was called into action.

"April 1886. 'J.H. Lane,' carrying molasses, sank. Seven out of 8 men survived."

" 'Georges Valentine,' carrying lumber. Five lost, 7 saved. Next day 'Cosme Colzada' runs aground three miles north of station. One dies in rigging."

The houses of refuge might never have been more than a footnote to history were it not for World War II. In 1942, German U-boats sank sixteen American merchant ships off the east coast of Florida. The houses of refuge, under control of the Navy, became submarine spotting stations and barracks for troops patrolling the coast for Nazi infiltrators.

Gilbert's Bar, by the way, is a shoal of rocks off Huntington Beach, not a place to go for Happy Hour. It was named after the pirate Don Pedro Gilbert, who roamed local waters aboard his ship *Panda* between 1820 and 1830.

Not the kind of fellow who would throw you a rope, we're betting.

Gilbert's Bar House of Refuge, now a museum, is open daily from 10:00 A.M. to 4:00 P.M. and is located at 301 S.E. MacArthur Blvd. in Huntington Beach, just east of Stuart. Phone (561) 225-1875. Admission is charged.

FLORIDA'S OLDEST RESTAURANT
Tampa

The sidewalk in front of Tampa's Columbia Restaurant is crowded with green historical markers, including one honoring Teddy Roosevelt and the Rough Riders, who passed through en route to the Spanish-American War in 1898. The most pertinent sign, though, proclaims the Columbia as the oldest restaurant in Florida.

Inside, diners may order a "1905 Salad," commemorating the year a cafe opened at the corner of Seventh Avenue and 23rd Street in Ybor City. That corner cafe, with its massive bar and dark wood furnishings, is still part of the Columbia. In newer parts of the restaurant, hand-painted tiles and murals decorate the walls and ceilings. Flamenco dancers perform two shows a night, with diners paying $6.00 extra to watch them stomp and swirl.

Over the years, celebrity guests have included everyone from Babe Ruth and Marilyn Monroe to the Rolling Stones and George Clooney.

Florida's oldest restaurant also might be its biggest and busiest. The Columbia can seat 1,600 guests in 11 dining rooms covering an entire city block. Each night the restaurant serves more than 400 of its famous salads; that's 150 heads of lettuce, 80 pounds of tomatoes, 50 pounds of cheese, and 8 gallons of dressing.

It's a long way from 1905 to "1905." A Cuban immigrant named Casimiro Hernandez founded the Columbia Restaurant. His son, Casimiro Jr., expanded the place and added the first air-conditioned dining area in Tampa. His daughter, Adela, and

CESAR GONZMART
MARCH 6, 1920
DECEMBER 9, 1992

"HE LIVED"

It's not every day that a classically trained violinist becomes a restaurant
entrepreneur. But Cesar Gonzmart did just that. Columbia Restaurant,
Florida's oldest, memorializes his contributions to its growth.

her husband, a classical violinist named Cesar Gonzmart, survived lean years in Ybor City before rebounding and expanding
to five locations in Florida.

A fourth generation of the Gonzmart family now runs the
Columbia, with a fifth generation on the way, and centennial
celebrations looming in 2005.

The Columbia Restaurant is at 2117 East Seventh Avenue,
Tampa. For more information, call (813) 248–4961. Hours are
11:00 A.M. to 10:00 P.M. Monday through Thursday, 11:00 A.M. to
midnight Friday and Saturday, and noon to 9:00 P.M. on Sunday.

YBOR CITY'S CIGAR-ROLLING HISTORY
Tampa

In party-hearty Ybor City, where hundreds of young people
dance and drink each weekend, it's easy to overlook the rare
history of the place. Look beyond the crowds, past the daiquiri
bars and nightclubs, and imagine a unique cigar-making community at the turn of the twentieth century.

Don Vincente Martinez Ybor (pronounced *E-bore*) opens a
cigar-rolling factory and builds a company town. Several thousand people—Cubans and Spaniards, Germans and Italians—
form their own social clubs, cultural organizations, and New
World traditions. There are cafes and streetcars, cigar ware-
houses and shotgun-style houses, labor strife and mutual aid
societies.

This heritage could hardly be more rich and flavorful.

The best place to begin exploring that history might be the 1905 Columbia House Restaurant on Seventh Avenue—Avenida Setima. Try having lunch in the dark corner bar that is part of the original establishment.

Your next stop might be on Ninth Street, the Ybor City State Museum, which is housed in the old Ferlita Bakery. The museum's not very big, but the story it has to tell carries you right through a brief visit. The best part might be a videotape history that includes interviews with old cigar rollers and natives of the area.

The namesake of the city was a native of Spain who'd founded his own cigar factories in Havana and then Key West. Ybor sought to solve the labor unrest and transportation problems by moving to Tampa, where a railroad line had been completed in 1884. His skilled workers could buy shotgun-style houses with monthly payments, and this stable, home-owning population helped make Ybor City grow. A few of these simple homes, known as casitas, have been moved beside the Ybor museum, and they're worth a look too.

A compelling part of Ybor history is the tradition of the lector, or reader, in the cigar factory. This man, paid by his fellow workers, would sit on a platform and read aloud while everyone else rolled cigars. In the mornings he'd report current events from newspapers and magazines. In the afternoons he'd act out the great novels of Cervantes, Zola, and Hugo.

It's hard to imagine such a scene, so different and rare in Florida history, but the Ybor City museum is the place to try.

The Ybor City State Museum, 1818 Ninth Avenue, Tampa, is open from 9:00 A.M. to 5:00 P.M. daily, except for major holidays. Admission is $2.00. Call (813) 247–6323 for more information.

SPONGE DIVING FOR DOLLARS
Tarpon Springs

A few years ago, Tarpon Springs High School made the *Late Night with David Letterman* show for a Top Ten list of ridiculous school nicknames: The Spongers.

No, they're not a bunch of cheapskates. The name was chosen to reflect the maritime history of this Gulf Coast city. At the turn of the twentieth century, a Greek community grew around the business of harvesting natural sponges from the shallow waters off Tarpon Springs, "the Sponge Capital of the World." The industry thrived north of Tampa Bay until the 1940s, when the sponge beds were destroyed by bacteria and artificial sponges entered the market. Only in the 1980s, when healthy beds were found, did the area once again become a leader in natural sponge harvesting.

Today the sponge docks remain busy with tourists, who stop by the many Greek restaurants and tourist attractions such as the Spongeorama, which has achieved something of a cult status. For $1.00, it offers a tour and a quaint old film showing how divers hook sponges and send them to the surface.

The festival highlight each year is the January 6 Epiphany Celebration, which includes a procession to Spring Bayou. This is where a local Greek Orthodox priest tosses a cross into the water and local boys dive for it, with the winner earning Tarpon Springs fame and good fortune.

For more information, call the Tarpon Springs Chamber of Commerce at (727) 937–6109.

A DRIVE-BY TRAPEZE ACADEMY
Venice

Along the Gulf Coast, where a sunset or a sidewalk sale is enough to disorient some drivers, there can be no greater distraction than the Tito Gaona Trapeze Academy. It's located just off of US 41 on the island of Venice, and tourists and retirees do double takes at the somersaults some students attempt while swinging 30 feet in the air.

Practice often begins at 5:00 P.M. on weekdays, just when most Venetians are driving past the flying trapeze.

"Sometimes people pull over and watch," says Chris Accardi, a fifty-one-year-old student and a clerk at the Sarasota County Tax Collector's Office. "It's good, it's kind of fun. When I see somebody I know, they'll wave."

Gaona, a fifty-three-year-old native of Guadalajara, Mexico, performed with the Ringling Bros. and Barnum & Bailey Circus for seventeen years. (He was also married for a while to Lee Meriwether, the actress who appeared in *Barnaby Jones* and *Circus of the Stars* on TV.) Gaona started the trapeze school beside his house in Venice, then moved to the former winter home of "The Greatest Show on Earth."

Now Gaona and his brother have established trapeze schools in Louisiana and California too. He dreams that it will catch on as adventurous exercise, wall climbing for the new millennium. In Venice, his students have been as young as six and as old as seventy-five. Some are more serious than others.

Accardi joined the school, bought a practice bar to use at home, and drives along US 41 to practice twice a week. "It's challenging and a good workout," she says. "And I love the reaction of people when I tell them I do the trapeze."

The Tito Gaona Trapeze Academy is located at 432 Spadero Drive, Venice. For information on lessons, call (941) 488–2496.

LITTLE ODESSA OF THE GULF COAST
Warm Mineral Springs

Florida has plenty of springs, but only one Warm Mineral Springs, where the water is always 87 degrees and the bathers are nearly always Eastern European. Call it Little Odessa on the Gulf Coast.

In a round pond about 50 yards across, Poles paddle beside Croats, and Lithuanians linger next to Ukrainians. Everyone seems stout and sturdy, soaking up both mineral water and the Florida sunshine. A typical conversation sounds something like "Przlovk dryz gblwick—Everglades, yah."

Hardly any Americans dip into the south Sarasota County spring, which is rich in minerals and has a distinctive sulfur smell. Florida archaeologists have dived into Warm Mineral Springs, though, and in 1977 it was listed as a significant site by the National Register of Historic Places. It seems that about 10,000 years ago, during the Paleo-Indian Period, animals such as mammoths and giant sloths gathered around the springs. Native American hunters also frequented the area. Bones and bone tools have been preserved in a debris cone 150 feet below the surface.

For most foreign visitors, this is ancient history. For them, the spring simply offers relaxation and a putative cure. Bathers mill around the shallow edges of the spring, moving in a clockwise direction. This isn't a European sense of direction, however. The spring water tends to swirl slowly clockwise, and people go with the flow.

Warm Mineral Springs, just north of North Port on US 41, is open from 9:00 A.M. to 5:00 P.M. daily. Admission is $7.00 for adults, $4.50 for students, and $2.00 for children under twelve. Also offered are massages and sauna treatments. For more information, call (941) 426–1692.

M ERMAIDS FOREVER
Weeki Wachee Springs

M ore than fifty years ago, in the days B.D.—Before Disney—a former Navy frogman named Newton Perry
opened his Mermaid Theatre north of Tampa at Weeki Wachee
Springs. Pretty young women with shimmering hair and glam-
orous costumes performed ballets and variety shows in the
crystal-clear spring water. It seems all too quaint now, but at
the time this was a breathtaking twist on the swimming performances of movie star Esther Williams.

Beverly Orchard, now a YMCA fitness director in Bradenton,
Florida, performed at the springs as an eighteen-year-old in
1956. Even today, half a century later, being a Weeki Wachee
mermaid means something.

"That's my story; everybody's interested in that," Orchard
says, laughing. "It was fun, a great adventure; I'd never been
away from home before. It had its glamour points, but it was
also hard work. I could go two minutes [holding her breath],
but you work up to that. You get very comfortable underwater."

Orchard still teaches swimming and water aerobics, and
goes scuba diving whenever she gets a chance. Once a mermaid, always a mermaid.

At a fiftieth anniversary in 1997, several generations of mer-
maids gathered for a reunion and "Tales of Yesteryear" performances in Weeki Wachee. Performers didn't make a lot of
money, and some lived in a mermaid dorm, but they all enjoyed
a one-of-a-kind experience.

The underwater shows go on even today, but it's not the same.

Weeki Wachee Springs is open from 10:00 A.M. to 3 P.M.
Wednesday through Sunday. Admission is $12.95, $9.95 for
children. For more information, call (352) 596–2062.

YOU WANT CHEESE ON THAT CRACKER?

*T*here are two kinds of Florida crackers. There's the one that gets soggy in about thirty seconds when exposed to our humidity, and there's the other kind that can best be defined as a . . . as an . . . well, actually, it's hard to say exactly what a Florida cracker is or was.

There are several theories on the subject. One is that cracker comes from the Celtic word meaning braggart or loudmouth. That might apply to some modern crackers, but it doesn't accurately describe the crackers of the 1800s, who were mostly hardworking, self-reliant folks who seldom ventured out of the backwoods.

Another theory is that cracker comes from corncracking, the method used to grind corn for grits and cornmeal. In this sense, it would mean a person of rustic ways who can't afford anything more than the most basic of foods. There are lots of people living throughout the South then and now who might fit this definition, but cracker is applied almost exclusively to folks in rural areas of south Georgia and Florida.

The most widely accepted theory is that cracker comes from the sound of whips used to drive herds of cattle. Florida cattlemen of the 1800s cracked their whips often to round up cattle that had wandered off into the swamps or palmetto scrub.

While Florida cattlemen might be proud to be called crackers, other people would not, as the word has some unpleasant connotations. In many instances, cracker is a synonym for ignorant Southern bigot.

So you've got to be careful who you call a cracker. One person might thank you for noticing his self-reliance and pioneering spirit, but another might punch you in the nose.

TOP TEN THINGS YOU'LL NEVER HEAR A FLORIDA CRACKER SAY

10. *I'll take Shakespeare for $1,000, Alex.*

9. *You can't feed that to the dog.*

8. *Duct tape won't fix that.*

7. *No kids in the back of the pickup. It's just not safe.*

6. *Of course professional wrestling is fake.*

5. *Who's Richard Petty?*

4. *I'd prefer unsweetened tea, please.*

3. *Have you seen my new MP3 player?*

2. *I'd like my catfish poached rather than deep-fried, please.*

And the Number One thing you'll never hear a Florida Cracker say (drumroll, please):

1. *Checkmate.*

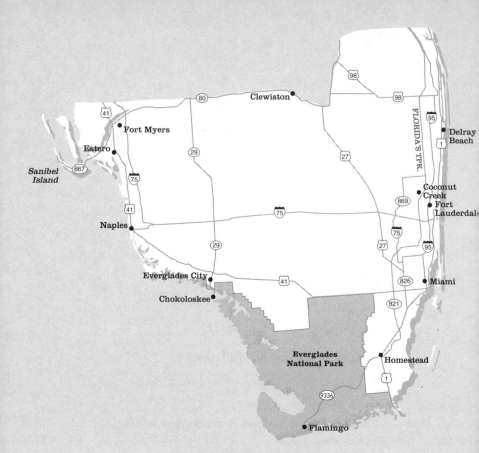

SOUTH FLORIDA

SOUTH FLORIDA

ISLAND RESTAURANT'S
THOUSAND-DOLLAR CEILING
Cabbage Key

At the Cabbage Key Inn and Restaurant, boaters leave tips on the table and dollar bills on the ceiling. The Charlotte Harbor tradition has caught on with tourists, and now signed and dated one-dollar bills paper the restaurant, covering the ceilings and walls, posts and tables.

Pale green George Washingtons stretch as far as the diner's eye can see, along with a bit of colorful cash in foreign currencies.

The story goes that years ago a local fisherman stuck a dollar bill on the Cabbage Key bar, as payment for a cold beer when he returned. These days there are hundreds of dollar bills, thousands of them, and they get taped and pasted on top of one another. Every few years the restaurant peels off all the bills and donates the money to charity.

Cabbage Key, a mere speck of land in the shallows of Pine Island Sound, is only accessible by boat. That's part of the island's quiet charm. Boaters and tour boaters stop by for a leisurely lunch, inside or out, where they can watch others come and go across the blue-green water.

The restaurant is supposed to have been the inspiration for Jimmy Buffett's "Cheeseburgers in Paradise," and there's an autographed photo of the singer above the bar. True or not, that's a nice story too.

Rooms on the island start at $65, with a two-night mini-
mum. The restaurant is open daily for breakfast, lunch, and
dinner; hours vary with the tourist season. For more information, call (941) 283–2278. If you don't have your own boat,
ferry tours from Pine Island include the Tropic Star. Call (941)
283–0015.

THE SMALLWOOD STORE AND KILLING MR. WATSON
Chokoloskee

Southeast of Naples, in the heart of what's called the Ten
Thousand Islands, lies the tiny town of Chokoloskee—"old
home" in the Seminole language. At the end of the road in
Chokoloskee is the Historic Smallwood Store, a Florida frontier
outpost and the setting for *Killing Mr. Watson,* Peter
Matthiessen's popular 1990 book. In it he tells the story of Wild
West outlaw Ed Watson, who claimed to have killed the infamous Belle Starr. Watson settled near Chokoloskee and quickly
set to feuding with his neighbors. Finally, after a 1910 hurricane, those neighbors shot him dead—right outside the Smallwood Store. Matthiessen deftly introduces historical characters
from the time to offer different points of view on Watson and
his misfortunes in the Ten Thousand Islands.

From a settler named Henry Thompson: "Nobody knew
where this man had come from, and nobody asked him. You
didn't ask a man hard questions, not in the Ten Thousand
Islands, not in them days. Folks will tell you different today,
but back then there wasn't too many in our section that wasn't

kind of unpopular someplace else. With all of Florida to choose from, who else would come to these overflowed, rain-rotted islands, with not enough high ground to build an outhouse, and so many skeeters plaguing you in the bad summers you thought you'd taken the wrong run straight to Hell."

Tourists today might enjoy a visit—if they're lathered in bug spray and leave before dusk, when the mosquitoes are thickest.

The Chokoloskee store was founded in 1906 by Ted Small-wood, who traded goods for plumes and hides brought in by Seminole hunters. In the years to come, local settlers would depend on the establishment for everything from patent medicines to the daily mail. The store made the National Register of Historic Places in 1974 and remained open until 1982. More recently, Smallwood's granddaughter reopened the store as the Ole Indian Trading Post and Museum, complete with a wax likeness of grandad. There are also dry goods and farm tools on display, along with the gator-hunting equipment of Loren "Totch" Brown, a lovable local rascal.

Brown was a World War II hero, gator poacher, and convicted marijuana smuggler who later showed Mathiessen around the Ten Thousand Islands. Then he wrote his own book, *Totch: A Life in the Everglades,* which described scratching out a living along Florida's final frontier.

Although he's no stylist, Brown could spin a yarn. He ended his book's introduction with a pledge of a poem:

> *While my writing is on the flow*
> *I'm going to write as though*
> *I'm still in the Everglades*
> *As hard as I can go*
> *Not only writing history*
> *But reliving it for you.*

For more information on the Smallwood Store, call (941) 695–2989.

AMERICA'S SWEETEST TOWN
Clewiston

Chances are that the sugar you put in your coffee every morning was once a tall piece of grass growing in the mucky soil south of Lake Okeechobee. Most of America's sugar is grown in counties surrounding the big lake and in the heart of it all is Clewiston, otherwise known as "America's Sweetest Town."

The sugar industry took off in the late 1920s after a couple of major storms caused widespread flooding, wiping out towns and farms. Political pressure was brought to bear, and soon the Army Corps of Engineers was shoring up the banks of Lake Okeechobee and digging canals to channel excess water south. Hundreds of thousands of acres of fertile cropland were created, much to the chagrin of modern environmentalists.

Stewart Mott of Mott's apple juice fame was designing cars for General Motors when he learned that a struggling sugar company near Clewiston was up for sale. He bought the company, which later became U.S. Sugar Corp., the largest sugar company in America.

If you've never seen sugarcane, it looks like a 15-foot high, thick-stalked blade of grass. The fields are set afire in October to burn off the foliage, then giant harvesters cut the cane. The stalks are sent to a mill where they are crushed, drained (they contain a lot of water), and refined into sugar or molasses.

The harvesting goes on twenty-four hours a day, seven days a week, for seven months. Christmas is the only day the great machines are silent.

There is, naturally, a Sugar Cane Festival, held every year in late April. Exhibits show the way sugar was made in the days before giant factories and machines. A high point of the day is the crowning of Miss Sugar Festival. Jeff Barwick, executive director of the Clewiston Chamber of Commerce, said they stopped choosing a Little Miss Sugar Festival because they weren't getting enough contestants. (Perhaps parents figured they had enough trouble controlling their kids' sweet tooth without getting them involved in something like that.)

There is also the Sweet Taste of Country Dessert Cooking Contest, featuring recipes that have to contain—can you guess?—sugar. The judges aren't inflexible, however. The 2001 Best Country Dessert recipe was a barbecue sauce.

For more information, call (863) 983-7979 or go to www.clewiston.org.

BUTTERFLIES ARE FINE, BUT THEY'RE NOT FREE
Coconut Creek

At Butterfly World, the only thing more remarkable than the ticket price ($15!) is the fact that it might actually be worth it. Where else would you get a chance to walk through an aviary thick with butterflies of every color and description? Kids love it, oohing and ahhing all over the place, and they just might learn something from the educational exhibits illustrating the life cycle of lepidoptera.

Paths wind through thick foliage as classical music plays faintly through the loudspeakers. Every minute or so an automatic mister surprises people with a spritz of cool water droplets. Benches provide a place to sit and watch the butterflies land and take flight, land and take flight.

Butterfly World was founded by Ronald Boender, an electrical engineer and insect breeder who always had a fascination for butterflies. He modeled his huge Broward County attraction on smaller butterfly houses in the United Kingdom.

"This is his paradise," says Solange Hall, one of the park guides. She can remember when Butterfly World opened ("March of '88") and she can remember when she started ("April of '88.") She remains devoted to the place, and her favorites are the atlas moths.

"I play with them," she admits, "when no one's here."

Butterfly varieties range from the emerald swallowtail to the peacock, the pansy, the red rim, the common rose, and the rusty-tipped page. They are as beautiful as their names. Because the butterflies are so near and so plentiful, everyone gets to play close-up nature photographer. It's a simple matter to compose shots that would take extraordinary patience or luck in the real world.

Butterfly World is just west of the Florida's Turnpike, exit 69, at 3600 West Sample Road, Coconut Creek. Admission is $14.95 for adults and senior citizens, $9.95 for children; kids under three get in free. Hours are 9:00 A.M. to 5:00 P.M. Monday through Saturday, 1:00 to 5:00 P.M. on Sunday. Because butterflies are "solar-powered," viewing is best in the morning on sunny days. For more information, call (954) 977–4400.

VIRTUAL ANGLING FOR VIDEO FISH
Dania Beach

With more than 1,000 miles of coastline, along with countless lakes, rivers, and streams, Florida is a warm-weather fishing paradise. There isn't a lot, though, for the hydrophobic fisherman. If you happen to be afraid of water, as you'd expect, you're pretty much out of luck when it comes to hooking a big one.

Except at the International Game Fish Association Hall of Fame and Museum, where a fishing simulator allows visiting anglers to remain high and dry.

The $30 million Dania Beach museum, which opened in 1999, offers educational material and interactive exhibits on any and every aspect of fishing. The history program includes an Egyptian drawing from 2000 B.C. showing a man fishing with a pole. (The hieroglyphics aren't translated, but he's probably talking about the one that got away.) The interactive fun peaks with "The Catch," a state-of-the-art game that allows guests to "fish" for everything from bass and trout to marlin and sailfish.

The game fish are shown on a video monitor, but the rod and reel are, well, real. How hard guests pull back on the rod and how fast they turn the reel will determine how long it will take to pull in a striking, leaping, and fighting fish. After one is landed, the screen will flash something like "Congratulations, your marlin weighed 145 pounds." This is usually accompanied by applause and happy squeals.

"I guess the kids like it the best," says George Klein, an IGFA guide. "Look, here comes a birthday party. This morning we had 400 Boy Scouts."

After "The Catch," visitors can learn to tie spider hitches, Palomar knots, and fishing flies. They can have lunch at the nearby Islamorada Fish Company, and they can go shopping next door for a huge array of fishing, hunting, and boating supplies at the Bass Pro Shops Outdoor World.

Back at the interactive exhibit, Klein assures guests that the game is not rigged. Most players, but not all of them, manage to land their catch.

"It's hard to lose a fish," he says, laughing, "but it can be done. A little screen comes up that says 'Try again next time.'"

The International Game Fish Association Hall of Fame and Museum is at 300 Gulf Stream Way, Dania Beach 33004. The museum is open daily from 10:00 A.M. to 6:00 P.M. Admission is $4.99, $4.49 for seniors, and $3.99 for children; kids under three get in free. For more information, call (954) 922–4212.

JAPANESE ZEN MEETS BORSCHT BELT HUMOR
Delray Beach

At the Morikami Museum, there are Japanese gardens and nature trails, orchid displays and bonsai collections, tea ceremonies and origami demonstrations. Tile-roof buildings slope before lakes crossed by arched bridges. The overall effect of the place is one of grace and serenity, relief from the hectic urban sprawl of South Florida.

Even Florida natives are surprised to discover a century-old connection between Japan and south Florida. In 1905 a young man named Jo Sakai led a pioneering agricultural expedition to Boca Raton. He and his companions founded a farming community and social experiment called the Yamato Colony. The community did not thrive, however, and families moved away one by one.

But one colonist remained. George Sukeji Morikami continued to work as a farmer and agricultural expedition, eventually buying several hundred acres of land. In the 1970s, near the end of his life, he donated 200 acres to Palm Beach County and the state of Florida.

Today the Morikami Museum celebrates the culture of Japan and the history of a Japanese colony. There are classes and workshops in the Japanese language, ink painting, haiku, origami, bonsai, nature photography, and kite making. A museum store offers gift items from Japan, while a cafe serves home-style Japanese food and snacks.

At least a few times each year, the Morikami also features Hideko Zwick, the Japanese yenta of Delray Beach, a flower arranger who is part Asian artist and part Joan Rivers.

In a Morikama auditorium lecture for the Hatsume Fair, for instance, this Japanese lady manipulated plants and flowers into the most elegant and delicate shapes. At the same time, she kept up an earthy running patter that was as funny as it was politically incorrect. One extended riff described the spectacle of older men running after younger women, along with the merits and demerits of Jewish men, including her longtime husband.

"When I have to tell him to drop dead, I do it in Japanese," Zwick quipped. "He always says, 'I know what you're saying,' though."

Tasteful arrangements followed tasteless remarks, along with audience gasps and laughter. Just when they thought she couldn't go any further, she did. One drawn-out story chronicled the long life and sudden death of a dear friend.

"She didn't even tell me goodbye," Zwick concluded. "I can't believe she did that."

The Morikami Museum and Japanese Gardens are at 4000 Morikami Park Road, Delray Beach 33446. Hours are 10:00 A.M. to 5:00 P.M. Tuesday through Sunday; closed Mondays and national holidays. Admission is $4.25, seniors $3.75, ages six through eighteen $2.00, children under six get in free. For more information, call (561) 495–0233.

KORESHAN UTOPIAN COMMUNITY
Estero

Besides the natural beauty of the Estero River, along with prime canoeing and camping, the Koreshan State Historic Site presents the odd story of a utopian community led by a Chicago doctor and religious visionary named Cyrus Teed.

In 1894 Teed led a few dozen followers to Lee County, Florida, where they started a communal society that he promised would become the New Jerusalem, a city of ten million people. Teed took the name Koresh—Hebrew for Cyrus— and preached in favor of celibacy, sharing, and equal rights for women. Perhaps the oddest belief of his cult was in "cellular cosmogony," which held that the universe exists on the inside of the hollow sphere of the earth.

These Koreshans built a store, bakery, sawmill, and laundry, along with a founder's house and residence halls. They also created an art hall where members studied music, drama, and literature. When Teed died in 1908, his followers, expecting his resurrection, laid out his body on the art hall stage. Teed never rose, though, and county inspectors insisted something be done. So the Koreshans placed his body in a mausoleum and watched it, twenty-four hours a day, ready to greet him on his triumphant return.

Teed's body was finally washed away in a 1921 hurricane, but the Koreshan community survived until the last remaining residents left the property to the state in 1961. On the state park grounds is the grave of Hedwig Michel, one of the spiritual leaders of the sect. Her epitaph: BE ASHAMED TO DIE UNTIL YOU HAVE WON SOME VICTORY FOR HUMANITY.

The Koreshan State Historic Site, just south of Fort Myers, offers nature trails, canoe rentals, and RV and tent camping along the Estero River. There are also the buildings of the Koreshan religious settlement established in 1894. Admission is $3.25 per vehicle. The state park is at US 41 and Corkscrew Road in Estero, off Interstate 75, exit 19. For more information, visit www.dep.state.fl.us/parks or call (941) 992–0311.

EVERGLADES SAFARI, SEMINOLE STYLE
Everglades

The Billie Swamp Safari offers a gung-ho glimpse of the Everglades, complete with airboat tours, meals in the Swampwater Cafe, and nights in authentic chickee huts with thatched palm roofs. It's billed as ecotourism, Seminole style, but it's more like an old-fashioned Florida tourist attraction. The whole complex reflects the rollicking style of James Billie, former Seminole chairman, Vietnam veteran, airplane pilot, tribal entrepreneur, and the most colorful of Florida characters.

Just two years ago, Billie, 57, decided to wrestle an alligator for the first time in more than a decade. That entertainment cost him an appendage, but not his sense of humor or his love of gators.

"He bit my hand," Billie quipped after surgery, "so I gave him my finger."

The setting for the Swamp Safari is the prairie edge of the Everglades, midway between Naples and Fort Lauderdale. Between grassy swamp and cypress woods, the Seminoles have carved out a rustic resort. The water route of the airboat tour, for instance, was gouged out by bulldozers, leaving piles of earth along the way. Alligators in this man-made pond are tossed food pellets to bring them closer to the boats. Guests are given earplugs to help dull the engine noise that scares away much of the wildlife native to the area.

Most of the park employees are white or Hispanic, and the young tour guides are more fun than informative. One worldly ecotourist from Washington, D.C., described the Safari experience as "Greenpeace meets the World Wrestling Federation."

Besides the gator-wrestling area, there are Florida panthers on display, along with a petting zoo and snake and reptile exhibits. A gift shop offers tribal souvenirs of every description. The Swampwater Cafe deep-fries everything from frog legs to gator tails, and there's storytelling around a campfire in the evening. Kids love the place.

The different huts that make up the park compound are called chickees. Their cypress wood frames are made of pressure-treated wood these days, but the palm roofs are layered and crisscrossed in the traditional manner. Just outside the main park area, there's a line of small chickee cabins that extends into a stand of cypress trees. The huts are plain and simple, with oil lamps, wire cots, and screened doors and windows. Their thatched roofs blend right into the landscape.

In the evening, after the last airboat tour roars by, there's the blessed quiet of the Everglades.

Swamp tours and rustic accommodations are available at the Seminole tribe's Big Cypress Reservation midway between Naples and Fort Lauderdale. Take Interstate 75 to exit 14, then drive 19 miles north on State Road 833.

Twenty-minute airboat rides are $12; hour-long swamp buggy tours are $20. Chickee huts for two rent for $35 a night. Larger thatched dorm huts sleep six, have ceiling fans and electric lights, and go for $65. For more information, visit www.seminoletribe.com/safari or call (800) 949–6101.

SWAMP TOURS AND THE ORCHID THIEF
Everglades

I f tourists call ahead during the winter months, they might be able to join a monthly group on a wading tour of the Fakahatchee Strand State Preserve east of Naples. Some visi-

tors wear gaiters over their shoes, others simply duct-tape
their jeans to their socks, the better to keep off the swamp
muck and mud. Mike Owen, a hyperenthusiastic park biolo-
gist, has been known to lead groups through waist-deep water
in search of biological items of interest. (There is a 2,000-foot-
long boardwalk for the squeamish.)

The Fakahatchee Strand is basically a long, thin drainage
slough (pronounced *slew)* for the Big Cypress Swamp along the
western edge of the Everglades. This still-remote area is home
to endangered animals such as the Florida panther and rare
plants, including the ghost orchid.

Which brings us to *The Orchid Thief,* Susan Orlean's best-
selling 1998 book and now a movie starring Nicolas Cage and
Meryl Streep.

In her book, Orlean follows the story of John Laroche, a
near toothless orchid fanatic who's caught stealing rare and
protected plants. This is part of her portrait: "Laroche strikes
many people as eccentric. The Seminoles, for instance, have
two nicknames for him: Troublemaker and Crazy White Man.
Once, when Laroche was telling me about his childhood, he
remarked, 'Boy, I sure was a weird little kid.'" Orlean describes
the beauty of the Fakahatchee Strand, by and by, but in the end
she decides it's "icky."

The movie, written and directed by the people who made
Being John Malkovich, is almost an anti-Fakahatchee film. It
was filmed in Los Angeles, for the most part, and turns out to
be about the screenwriter's struggle to adapt the Florida book
to the Hollywood screen.

To see the Fakahatchee Strand for yourself, drive to
Copeland, north of Everglades City on State Road 29. The park
is open daily from 8:00 A.M. to sundown. Call (941) 695–4593.

THE TAMIAMI TRAIL AND ALLIGATOR ALLEY

South Florida's two main east-west highways, both crowded with cars today, began as dubious propositions, if not the objects of ridicule. The Tamiami Trail, which opened in 1928, crosses the Everglades between Tampa and Miami. That's how it got the name—get it? Predictably, some Tampa natives claimed this was unfair, that their city would get just two letters while Miami was spelled out in full.

When newcomers stumble over the name today, locals take a shortcut: They simply call it "41," as in US 41.

Alligator Alley, a toll road that's now part of Interstate 75, crosses the Big Cypress Swamp between Naples and Fort Lauderdale. When the highway was first suggested, this was the loneliest of routes, and a state legislator suggested only alligators would use the road. This, too, gained fame in a name.

VEGAS OF THE GLADES
Everglades

If you're driving east into Miami along US 41, emerging from the vast expanse of the Everglades, Miccosukee Bingo and Gaming looms over the landscape like some kind of giant pastel egret. The ten-story hotel-casino is a monument to bingo, slot machines, and the $6.95 steak-and-lobster special. The way it rises so abruptly from the natural wonder of the glades must be some sort of inside joke or tribal revenge.

The huge casino parking lot, ironically enough, offers animal-coded areas to help visitors remember where they left their cars. You can park in the heron section, for instance, which is no doubt where herons once lived before the marsh was paved over to make way for tour buses full of chain-smoking gamblers.

The design of the place is a pastiche—call it nuevo-retro-deco-modern—featuring fluted columns, yellow-green walls, and purple trim, along with pink sofas and fanciful easy chairs shaped like high-heeled shoes. Not that people notice, as they yank slot machine levers all day and night.

In the Emeek-Cheke restaurant, the menu offers both roasted snapper Mediterranean, at $17.95, and alligator tail Provençal, a bargain at $8.95. The second-floor lobby shows photos of tribal leaders such as Billy Cypress, but precious few tribal members seem to work at the casino or gamble there. There is a forlorn statue of a young Miccosukee boy in front of the hotel, though. He's holding a frog, looking off into the distance, and couldn't look more innocent.

Of course, he's got his back to the casino.

Miccosukee Bingo and Gaming, at Krome Avenue and US 41, is open 365 days a year. Call (305) 222–4653 for information.

THE END OF THE ROAD IN
THE EVERGLADES
Flamingo

If Flamingo isn't the most remote spot in Florida, then what is? Even the loneliest Panhandle town lies near enough to Interstate 10 and Pensacola or Tallahassee. Even the tiniest speck of the Florida Keys clings to well-traveled US 1 between Miami and Key West. Even the quietest Okeechobee village joins the thickening web of country roads that crisscross Central Florida.

No, this has to be it: Flamingo, population 65, a tiny gateway to Florida Bay hidden deep within Everglades National Park.

Most Floridians have never heard of the place, much less visited it. They have no idea what they're missing, either, because Flamingo is at once a company town, a natural wonder, and a godforsaken haunt for mosquitoes, mosquitoes, and more mosquitoes. It's only connected to the rest of the state by a 50-mile-long park road.

"Once you get to Flamingo, you're either going by water or by foot—and not very far by foot," said Peter Allen, a park naturalist. "This is the end of the road."

Even in 1938, nine years before Everglades National Park was dedicated, naturalists realized the area lacked the popular appeal of Yellowstone or the Grand Canyon. Dan Beard, the naturalist and illustrator who is credited with bringing scouting to America in the early 1900s, noted that "There are no knife-edged mountains protruding up to the sky. There are no valleys of any kind. No glaciers exist, no gaudy canyons, no geysers, no mighty trees unless we except the few royal palms, not even a rockbound coast with the spray of ocean waves. . . . To put it crudely, there is nothing (and we include the bird rookeries) in the Everglades that will make Mr. Jonnie Q. Public suck in his breath."

This is perhaps overstated—sunsets over Florida Bay are deservedly famous—but many visitors do find the Everglades underwhelming. Still, many park rangers and workers who have lived and worked at the Grand Canyon or Yellowstone have chosen to leave the grandeur of those places for what is essentially a South Florida swamp.

Some Flamingoans ride their bicycles to work through "Mosquito Alley," a mangrove shortcut from employee housing to the marina. At a certain speed, mosquitoes won't land on a biker. The only problem with maintaining this speed is that large alligators sometimes lie across the path to sun themselves.

One particular gator, a sorry old three-legged fellow, has suffered many hits and near misses. He has been given a nickname: Speed Bump.

During the winter tourist season, Flamingo opens an employee pub, the Wreck Hall, where the rest rooms are named Manatee and Womanatee. A weekly newsletter, *The Mullet Wrapper,* features bulletins, a humorous Mosquito Index, and the occasional employee squabble on the op-ed page. The marina store sells everything from $41 mosquito nets to 85-cent fly swatters, along with bumper stickers that read I GAVE BLOOD AT EVERGLADES NATIONAL PARK.

It would be very, very difficult to exaggerate the Flamingo mosquitos, particularly from April through October, the rainy season. Locals know better than to venture out unprotected at dawn and dusk, lest they return with dozens of welts and bloody splotches from the suckers they've managed to swat. A common sight is a Flamingo resident out walking his dog while wearing a mosquito-proof mesh jacket complete with gloves and hood.

An equally common sight is an unsuspecting visitor performing what's known as the "Flamingo Two-Step," frantically slapping at exposed arms and legs while spraying great clouds of insect repellent.

George O'Meara, a University of Florida entomologist in Vero Beach, said Flamingo just might be the buggiest place in Florida, if not the world. For years he studied the black salt marsh mosquito *(Aedes taeniorhynchus)* and journeyed to Flamingo to collect specimens. Professionally, it was paradise. Personally, he didn't like it any more than anyone else.

"This particular mosquito, when there are billions and billions of them, they're thick even in the middle of the day," O'Meara says. "In the mangrove swamp you can hear them for a second or two when they take wing, before they engulf you. When they're bad, in the evening, you can't open your mouth if you're talking to someone.

"You have to talk through your teeth or out of the side of your mouth. If you have to take a breath or something, you'll swallow several dozen easily."

SAVE THE LIFEGUARDS FROM THEIR STANDS!
Fort Lauderdale

In Fort Lauderdale, the city decided to replace rickety old wooden lifeguard stands with stylish new aluminum ones, to better reflect the beach community's posh image. The 2002 move was delayed, however, when officials decided the new stands were unsafe. Ramps leading up to the towers were too steep, and lifeguards complained that side windows did not open, making them unbearably hot.

"We're not putting lifeguards in them until they are completely safe," said beach patrol Lt. Breck Ballou.

In related news, the Fort Lauderdale Fire Department replaced fire poles with escalators to help prevent chafing. The

*Lifeguards had to be protected from their own
stands when Fort Lauderdale replaced the old
lifeguard stands with new ones in 2002.*

Fort Lauderdale Sanitation Department fought to have the rear
steps on garbage trucks replaced with La-Z-Boy recliners. And
the Fort Lauderdale Police Department refused to wear new
holsters because "they make us look fat."

Meanwhile, back at the beach, city officials have added hand
railings and traction bars to the ramps. Newer stand models
will have better ventilation too, so that lifeguards will feel more
comfortable. As part of a community response to the issue, Fort
Lauderdale nursing homes have volunteered to help. Residents
with walkers will escort lifeguards to emergencies at the
water's edge, and nurse's aides will help them climb back into
their stands after a rescue. New television sets with VCRs will
show continuous loops of old *Baywatch* reruns.

EDISON'S GREAT MIND AND QUIRKY CHARM
Fort Myers

At the Thomas Edison winter home in Fort Myers, guests can walk in the famous inventor's footsteps, filing past early light bulbs, batteries, and phonographs before learning some of the great man's quirks and charms, the gifts of an original mind.

The house Edison designed, for instance, was prefabricated in Maine before being shipped to the south bank of the Caloosahatchee River in 1886. What he called "Seminole Lodge" was practical, suited to pre-air-conditioned Florida, and had several interesting features. The electric chandeliers ("electroliers") were designed by Edison and built in his own shop. The kitchen and dining room are part of the guest house, because Edison suffered from stomach ulcers and didn't care for the smell of food cooking. Also, if his visitors proved tiresome, he could excuse himself after dinner and return to his own quarters, rather than having to wait for them to leave.

Edison's most famous guest was his friend and admirer Henry Ford, the automobile pioneer, who built his own winter home along the river in 1916. Both are part of the Edison-Ford Winter Estates, which offer tours every day but Christmas and Thanksgiving.

The wonders begin even before the tours start. Edison collected plants of all kinds, as part of his search for a natural source of rubber, and his friend Harvey Firestone gave him a banyan tree from southeast Asia in 1925. That tree is now the largest banyan in North America, measuring some 400 feet across, and it's threatening to take over a museum parking lot.

A guided tour includes what was a working research laboratory on the estate. There's a small cot where Edison, who didn't need much sleep, took catnaps during the day. After his death in 1931, workers had to test the chemicals he was using in the lab; the famous inventor, blessed with a prodigious memory, never needed to label bottles. He simply remembered what was in each one, year after year after year.

On the estate grounds, which include a friendship walk between the Ford and Edison homes, there's a swimming pool, one of the first in Florida, built with cement from Edison's cement company. Edison also had an electric boat on the river, but preferred to relax by fishing from the shore. To make he sure he wasn't disturbed, he wouldn't bait his hook.

Edison was completely deaf in his later years, and one of the most personalized exhibits in the museum is a family phonograph. It has teeth marks on a wooden edge where Edison would bite down on the wood and "listen" to the music through the vibrations in his jaw.

The Edison-Ford Winter Estates, at 2350 McGregor Boulevard in Fort Myers, are open for guided tours from 9:00 A.M. to 4:00 P.M. Monday through Saturday, and noon to 4:00 P.M. on Sunday. For more information, visit www.edison-ford-estate. com, or call (941) 334–3614.

DIAMONDS ARE STILL A GIRL'S BEST FRIEND
Homestead

Edward Leedskalnin was so in love with Agnes Scuffs that he built for her a house made out of coral.

Edward Leedskalnin was a romantic man—he
believed his fiancée would be impressed by a house
made of rock.

At the Coral Castle, the walls are made out of coral and the gates are made out of coral. There are coral rocking chairs, a coral bed, a coral table in the shape of a heart, coral fountains, and even a kind of coral stockade in case any children they might have (and maybe even Agnes) were ever in need of discipline.

One can only imagine what Ed would have built if he disliked Agnes.

Actually, it's all rather romantic, in a nineteenth-century Latvian sort of way. Ed was born in Latvia in 1887. When he was twenty-six, he was engaged to marry Agnes, ten years his junior. To his dying day, Ed referred to her as "Sweet Sixteen."

On the day before the wedding, Sweet Sixteen backed out on the grounds that Ed was too old for her. Ed believed there were other reasons, like the fact he had only a fourth-grade education, had no money, and enjoyed imprisoning children in coral stockades. Actually, we're making that last part up. We think.

Anyway, Ed's heart was broken by Sweet Sixteen's rejection, so he left Latvia and spent some time wandering around Canada and the United States working at lumber camps and driving cattle.

Somehow, these itinerant occupations gave Ed the incentive, skill, and determination to single-handedly dig out, move, and arrange twenty-nine-ton slabs of coral rock into a castle of unrequited love. The work was certainly not made any easier by the fact that Ed stood five feet tall, weighed one hundred pounds, and was plagued with bouts of tuberculosis.

For twenty years, from 1920 to 1940, Ed worked on the home for his bride who would never be. He worked alone, at night, by lantern light, first scraping off the 2 or 3 inches of topsoil that cover the 4,000-foot-thick coral bedrock that lies beneath this part of South Florida. Then, using hand tools fashioned from parts of old Model T Fords, he chiseled, pulleyed, levered, hoisted, and dragged the mammoth slabs of fossilized coral from as far away as Florida City, 10 miles to the south.

How did Ed, a little wheezing squirt of a man with an elementary-school education, assemble this 11,000-ton house, the South Florida equivalent of Stonehenge or the pyramids, all by himself? That is the essential and perhaps never-to-be-answered riddle of Coral Castle. There are no pictures, written records, or eyewitnesses to the construction. A few rotting implements in his "toolshed" are the only clues.

Ed, as you've probably surmised by now, was kind of a weird guy. Besides laboring under a Fred Flintstone–like delusion that chicks dig sleeping on beds made of rock, Ed was convinced that there are "energy lines" running between the north and south poles that can be harnessed by six-pointed Latvian "lucky stars," several of which adorn the walls and furniture of Coral Castle.

Ed was a hermit by night but gregarious by day. He built high, thick walls to shield his work from the eyes of strangers, yet he'd let children visit during the daytime for 10 cents a head. (Ed also threw in a complimentary hot dog, steamed in an old Model T differential. Today, adults are charged $9.75 admission, franks not included.)

The Coral Castle story is inspiring, but also rather sad. Ed died in Miami in 1954 at the age of sixty-four. Despite repeated entreaties, the love of his life, Sweet Sixteen, never paid a single visit.

Coral Castle is located at 28655 South Dixie Highway in Homestead. Phone (305) 248-6345 or connect to the Web site at www.coralcastle.com. There are guided tours daily; admission is charged.

CASA DE ELIAN
Miami

In Little Havana, along Eighth Street—Calle Ocho—English will get you nowhere. Visitors must rely on what they learned, or tried to learn, in Spanish 101. Fortunately, the necessary question is a simple one:

"Donde esta la casa de Elian?"

Everyone will know you mean Elian Gonzalez, the little Cuban boy caught in a custody battle that became an international affair. Everyone will offer you directions, and most of those directions will take you toward Flagler Street and then Second Street, N.W., where Elian lived for five months.

The Gonzalez family has turned the site into a shrine called Unidos en Casa Elian, or the United in Elian House.

In Miami's Little Havana, the house where Elian Gonzalez
stayed is now a shrine and is open to the public on Sundays.

It's a little stucco home with big Cuban and American flags
out front. A 4-foot-tall crucifix is set on a wall, and there's a
poster-size photograph of the boy on the front door. To the side
is a small swing set and wooden sign that reads EL PARQUE DE
ELIAN.

At the front gate is a shrine to his mother, Elizabeth, who
died on the fateful boat trip that brought him to Florida. Beside
it on a chain-link fence are posted heartfelt and handwritten
testimonials. One begins "Con mi sangre escribo . . ." or "With
my blood I write . . ."

Elian Gonzalez was rescued from the Atlantic Ocean 2 miles off of Fort Lauderdale on Thanksgiving Day 1999. Miami relatives took him in, but his father back in Cuba wanted custody. The Gonzalez family refused, and there was a high-profile standoff for weeks, with anti-Castro activists crowding the street outside the house. Elian was finally reunited with his father after U.S. Border Patrol agents raided the home before dawn on April 22, 2000.

The Second Street shrine was opened to the public for free visits in November 2001. A Spanglish sign on the front door offers Sunday visiting hours: HORARIOS: 10 A.M.–6 P.M.

Inside, the house is filled with dozens of Elian photos, along with clothes, toys, and paraphernalia. One poster calls him "The Miracle Child," while another shows the Pulitzer Prize–winning photo of an armed federal agent taking him from the house.

Next door to the shrine, a media-weary neighbor watches people come and go. Some visitors stop to take pictures, or place candles and flowers, while others go inside for the full tour. It can get busy.

"*A veces,*" the man says with a shrug—"Sometimes."

JAI-ALAI'S FADED GLORY
Miami

It's hard to believe, surveying the seedy grandeur of Miami Jai-Alai, but this game once had cachet. Beginning in the 1920s, high-society couples attended sold-out matches in dress suits and evening gowns. First Lady Eleanor Roosevelt attended a performance, and later on the matches were shown on local television. The Miami arena, or fronton, was known as "The Yankee Stadium of Jai-alai."

Today the game remains the same, a fascinating cultural artifact from the Basque region of Spain, but the scene has changed.

The Miami fronton is now located in the industrial park limbo that is "near the airport." It's the kind of place where you park in the lot, and then double-check to make sure your doors are locked. Inside, the stands reek of cigarette smoke, most of the seats are empty, and it's the rare leaping play that draws approving calls from the crowd. More common is energetic, multilingual cussing when bettors play their hunches and lose, or when a lucky number fails to fall into place.

Still, the place has a certain down-at-the-heels charm, and it might be the perfect antidote to a day at Disney World.

Jai-alai—pronounced *high-lie* (it means "merry festival" in Basque)—certainly is different, practically unique to Florida in the United States. Five of the nation's six frontons are here, in Dania, Fort Pierce, Ocala, Orlando, and Miami. The Miami arena is the largest, with 6,000 seats, and the oldest, built in 1926. It features American and Basque players who go by marvelous one-word names such as Areitio, Lejardi, and Zumaya. When a game comes down to the final point, and fans are shouting out encouragement, the fronton doesn't seem so jaded.

The sport is sometimes billed as "the world's fastest game," because players can hurl a ball, or pelota, at speeds greater than 150 miles per hour. Jai-alai is played on a three-sided court, and players must use a curved basket, or cesta, to catch the ball and fling it back against the front wall in one fluid motion.

It's a little like racquetball, only much cooler.

Because most fans are more interested in gambling than in the game itself, the state lottery has hurt attendance and forced several frontons out of business. Today the fronton offers large-screen televisions so gamblers can follow their bets on everything from football to Thoroughbred and harness racing.

It's hard to believe the game will rebound and regain its former glory, but who knows? It's a long shot, but so is winning a superfecta bet, and jai-alai fans take those odds every day.

Miami Jai-Alai is located at 3500 NW 37ᵗʰ Avenue. Programs are $1.00, and the minimum bet is $2.00. Call (305) 633–6400 for match times.

W ORLD C HESS H ALL OF F AME
M i a m i

First, a quiz. The Ruy Lopez opening is *(a)* the hottest new Floribbean restaurant on Miami Beach, *(b)* a Menudo-inspired dance move that Ricky Martin is bringing back on tour, or *(c)* a classic gambit to begin a chess match.

If you know *C* is the correct answer, then the new World Chess Hall of Fame in Miami might be worth a visit. It's just off the Florida Turnpike, near Miami MetroZoo, in a fanciful building with chessboard squares and a 45-foot-tall tower that looks like a castle.

If you don't know a rook from a hole in the ground, of course, then the World Chess Hall of Fame might be the last place in Miami to visit. You'll probably find that the only exhibit more boring than the *History of Chess Literature and Periodicals* is the *History of Rating Systems and Chess Notations.* Zzzzzz, indeed.

Maybe that's the real future of the place, as a threat to the misbehaving children of Florida tourists: "Now, kids, we've been to the beach, and the outlet mall, and a baseball game, and you've done nothing but complain! If you don't straighten up, and I mean right now, we're going straight to the World Chess Hall of Fame!"

The Hall of Fame and Sidney Samole Chess Museum are associated with Excalibur Electronics, a company that makes computer chess games. There's even a sword stuck in a rock outside the front door, following the Arthurian legend. Museum employees doubt that any visitor will be able to pull it loose.

Inside, the museum does what it can with the contemplative game of chess. A dark, spooky entryway offers a history lesson dating back to Arab and Indian origins of the game. There is a chess film, along with a display that re-creates the famous match between Boris Spassky and Bobby Fischer. A gift shop offers *Star Trek* and *Star Wars* chess games, along with, inexplicably, a version with pieces modeled on characters from *The Simpsons*. (Exactly how savvy can a Homer piece be?)

At the grand opening of the museum on December 16, 2001, an outdoor chess game featured actors in medieval dress, along with a simultaneous chess exhibition by a few grand masters. Inside, a crowd of preteen boys played a rowdy game of team chess with foot-high pieces set on the museum floor. They called out moves, bickered back and forth, and even indulged in a little strategic trash talking.

"I can taste it," crowed one boy, nearing checkmate, "and it tastes good."

The World Chess Hall of Fame and Sidney Samole Chess Museum is at 13755 S.W. 119th Avenue, Miami. Admission is $5.00 for adults, $3.00 for children. Hours are 1:00 to 8:00 P.M. on Thursday, 10:30 A.M. to 5:00 P.M. on Friday and Saturday, and 1:00 to 5:00 P.M. on Sunday. Call (305) 477–8080, or visit www.worldchesshalloffame.com.

SEMINOLE STATEMENT OF 1936

After more than a century of war, deprivation, and relocation to reservations, the Seminoles of Florida wanted no part of dealing with the United States of America. In 1936, state officials organized a Seminole Conference near Monroe Station in the Everglades east of Naples. Tribal spokesmen were wary, though, and told the governor they wanted only one thing. "Pohoan chekish," they said. Leave us alone.

I'LL PUT $3.00 ON GLASS SECRETARIAT
Naples

People call Craig Colquhoun the "glass horsey man" and, believe it or not, he doesn't mind.

That's because Colquhoun (pronounced *cole-HUNE*) has a dream that involves lots of horses and lots of glass. He wants to build a glass version of Churchill Downs, home of the Kentucky Derby. There will be glass horses, glass viewing stands, flapping glass flags, and the familiar twin spires of the grandstand. Made of glass, of course.

Glass artist Craig Colquhoun gets by making sculptures of golfers and horses until he can complete his grand vision of an all-glass Churchill Downs.

Also glass people. About 100,000 of them. All handmade.

The glass artist from Newcastle, England, figures he has the skill to pull off this mammoth project, which he estimates will take two years to complete and will fill the inside of a three-car garage. All he needs is the money to do it, about $200,000.

"I want to be careful who I get involved with financially because I don't want to lose creative control," the artist said from his Polar Art Glass studio in a Naples industrial park.

Colquhoun has warmed up for his masterpiece by building a glass tennis stadium that bears a slight resemblance to Wimbledon, glass Harley-Davidson motorcycles, glass ships-in-bottles, glass sharks, glass golfers, and a glass re-creation of New York City firemen raising the American flag at Ground Zero.

Always in the back of his mind as he works on these smaller projects is Churchill Downs. After winning a grant from the Prince of Wales Trust, a meeting with Princess Diana in 1986 convinced him he should do whatever it takes to achieve his dream.

"What we talked about was my desire to do something big," he said. "She told me to follow my dream, and that's what I'm doing."

Colquhoun, 39, will make a glass Churchill Downs with the same tools he uses to make trophies and Christmas ornaments. He heats Pyrex tubes and rods with a propane and oxygen torch, then blows and bends the glass into whatever shape he desires.

As obsessed as he is, Colquhoun didn't start out wanting to be a glass artist. He wanted to be a professional soccer player, but the wiry center-forward never made it. Looking for a way to make a living, he was taken under the wing of a Newcastle glassblower twenty-five years ago and quickly learned the trade. He came to America three years ago to make his Churchill Downs vision a reality.

As we spoke, some ominous sound of cracking glass issued from the back of Coquhoun's studio.

"Oh, that's nothing," he said. "Just a stress fracture. Happens whenever the temperature changes."

It would be interesting to see if his attitude is quite so cavalier if and when 100,000 glass horse-racing fans suddenly feel a chill.

Craig Colquhoun's Polar Art Glass studio/showroom is located at #1, 4601 Enterprise Avenue, Naples. Phone (941) 436-6678 or visit his Web site at www.polarartglass.com.

TEDDY BEARS, TEDDY BEARS, AND MORE TEDDY BEARS
Naples

Beary near downtown Naples, and bearly west of Interstate 75, there's a place that just might be the beary cutest on the Gulf Coast. You'll have to bear with fans of the Teddy Bear Museum of Naples, because a visit with more than 3,000 stuffed animals might leave you teddy-talking until your buttonlike eyes are set in a fixed position.

There's a teddy here for every taste, from antique and limited edition bears to new and avant garde bears. There are teddy bears from twenty-eight countries. There are teddy bears made of wood and crystal, marble and bronze. There are teddy bear posters, paintings, and sculptures. With considerable pride, the museum bills itself as "The Most Comprehensive Collection of Bears in North America!"

The fuzzy Naples museum opened in 1990 when Frances Pew Hayes donated the hundreds of bears in her private collection. She'd become an arctophile, or teddy bear lover, after receiving one as a birthday gift from a grandson.

Fans are invited to "paw through" the museum Web site, www.teddymuseum.com, which features a mind-altering loop of music from the old "Teddy Bear Picnic" radio show. There's also a museum mission statement, which is provided here in its entirety:

"To promote the understanding of the history and uses of artist and manufacturer teddy bears as a positive force in the world and lives of children of all ages. To improve and enrich the lives of all children of all ages through education about bears, sharing the joy and enthusiasm of and for teddies, using teddies to entertain and promote caring and warmth to those in need of physical and mental comfort. To promote the appreciation and recognition of bear making as a soft sculpture art form. To display teddy bears and related items for the enjoyment and information of children of all ages."

Amid the concrete sprawl that is Naples, the nonprofit museum stands apart in a shady stand of pine trees. Inside, besides all the teddy bear displays, there's a library of books and a gift shop with all sorts of bearaphernalia.

After a visit, guests are free to hibernate.

The Teddy Bear Museum of Naples, at 2511 Pine Ridge Road, is open from 10:00 A.M. to 4:00 P.M. Tuesday through Saturday, closed Sunday and Monday. Admission is $6.00 for adults, $4.00 for seniors, and $2.00 for children over the age of four. For information, call (866) 365–BEAR.

THE COUNTRY'S SMALLEST POST OFFICE
Ochopee

Tiny, buggy Ochopee, which is hardly a bump on a road in the Everglades, has become a pilgrimage of sorts for philatelists from across the country and around the world. Stamp collectors, you see, crave letters with a postmark from what's believed to be the nation's smallest post office.

It's hard to imagine a smaller one, because the Ochopee Post Office looks little bigger than an outhouse. Considering the time-honored use of the Sears catalog, and the modern proliferation of junk mail, this may be considered social commentary.

The tin-roofed and white-painted hut sits on a curve in US 41, the old Tamiami Trail highway, about an hour southeast of Naples. There's a flagpole to one side of the building, and a picnic table to the other, with a gravel parking lot for cars to circle. A green historical marker, which is almost bigger than the office itself, explains the history of the place.

It seems that the building was once an irrigation pipe shed for the J. T. Gaunt Company tomato farm. After a night fire burned down the old Ochopee general store and post office in 1953, the shed was pressed into service by postmaster Sidney Brown. It's been in use ever since, still serving local families and the stamp fans who drop off mail to collect postmarks.

UPS and Federal Express, presumably, aren't interested in challenging this monopoly.

"*NUDE EVERGLADES*" *GALLERY*
Ochopee

Visitors to Ochopee tend to stop across the street from the Smallest Post Office to visit Joanie's Blue Crab Cafe, which is becoming an attraction in its own right.

The timeworn cafe dates back to the 1930s, when it was a storage building for the Standard service station next door. Now the gas station is closed, and the shed offers snacks, meals, and rest rooms "for patrons only." A soda sells for $1.50, with $2.95 key lime pie and $10.95 soft-shell crab sandwiches. The musty place is filled with souvenirs, paintings for sale, and poetry for everyone to share:

Mosquito, mosquito, why do you sting?
Such a big pain, from a little thing!

Mosquito, mosquito, I can get you with a smack,
But your billions of relatives keep coming back!

You can read other such poems in one of the Blue Crab's rest rooms. The other rest room is less literary and more, um, graphic. Its walls are covered with framed photographs of half-nekkid local women posed outdoors. A few of them wear thongs at the beach, or embrace pickup trucks, while another is draped only in a Confederate flag.

Southern soft-core. Skeeter porn. Playglades.

When asked about this gallery, the store manager laughs and explains that it's part of the "Nude Everglades" portfolio of an Ochopee amateur photographer. This guy takes pictures of his wife and other local women, and goes by the name "Lucky."

Well, he'd have to be.

Joanie's Blue Crab Cafe can be found at 39395 Tamiami Trail, Ochopee. It's open from 11:00 A.M. to 5:00 P.M. in summer and 11:00 A.M. to 8:00 P.M. in winter. It's a good idea to call first and check on the hours. Depending on how busy they are, the cafe sometimes closes sooner or later than its official hours. Phone (941) 695–2682.

THE SHELL FACTORY AND "THE SANIBEL STOOP"

Sanibel Island

If you look at a map of Florida's Gulf Coast, you'll notice that most of the coastal keys are long, thin islands that follow the shoreline north and south. The exception to that rule is Lee County's Sanibel Island, which is an east-west crescent swinging out into the Gulf of Mexico.

That's why there are so many seashells on the island, especially after tropical storms move up the coast. The popular island sport is called "shelling" by locals and tourists alike, and there's even a name for the position assumed by so many shellers: "The Sanibel Stoop."

Local shell history and literary notables include Anne Morrow Lindbergh, wife of the famous aviator and author of *Gift from the Sea,* the 1955 best-seller. She wrote the book on Captiva Island, which extends north of Sanibel. *Gift from the Sea* uses different seashells as a launching point for meditations on love and marriage, peace and happiness.

Today, on the mainland of Lee County, in North Fort Myers, there's the profoundly unmeditative Shell Factory, where nautical treasures meet the mass market of tourism. In this 75,000-square-foot complex, thousands of samples of thousands of seashells fill yard after yard of exhibit space. There are common and rare shells, ranging from *Telescopium* (3 for $1.00) to *Cypraea valentia* ($4,000 apiece). Only 5 percent of the inventory is domestic, with the rest coming from fifty countries around the globe.

Souvenirs include shell-encrusted novelties, dolls, and lamps made in Taiwan and the Philippines. Then there are beach towels, snorkels, and the usual Florida bric-a-brac, along with a growing section of Christmas decorations and novelties. Finally, for when families are shelled and shopped out, there are concessions, wildlife exhibits, and bumper boat rides.

By then they'll be ready to return to the quiet shelling of Sanibel Island.

The Shell Factory is at 2787 North Tamiami Trail, North Fort Myers. Call (941) 995–2141 for more information.

WHO PUT THE "DING" IN DING DARLING?
Sanibel Island

irders know the call, and its meaning, but tourists might be forgiven for assuming that the words *Ding Darling* announce cocktail hour at exclusive resorts on the Florida Gulf Coast.

Even locals might be surprised to learn that J. N. "Ding" Darling, namesake of the National Wildlife Refuge on Sanibel Island, began his career with a poison pen. His political cartoons won two Pulitzer Prizes and appeared in more than 150 newspapers in the early 1900s. Later on he became better known as a sportsman and conservationist, the founder of the National Wildlife Federation, and a pioneer who fought for the preservation of habitat throughout Florida.

If all this information isn't enough to win bar bets and trivia contests, go with this one: Darling was known as "Ding" to everyone, but the J. N. stood for Jay Norwood.

The J. N. "Ding" Darling National Wildlife Refuge is at One Wildlife Drive, off Sanibel-Captiva Road. Admission is $5.00 per automobile, $1.00 for pedestrians and cyclists. For more information, call (941) 472–1100.

THE WORLD'S LARGEST DRIVE-IN
Sunrise

here are thirty-two outdoor movie screens in Florida, and more than a third of them are at the Thunderbird Drive-In near Fort Lauderdale. It's the mother of all drive-ins, the largest in the United States, and a big fat slice of Americana. If drive-ins are dinosaurs, a dying breed, then the Thunderbird is *Jurassic Park*—and *Jurassic Park II* and *Jurassic Park III*.

The Thunderbird is no nostalgia house catering to aging baby boomers, though. It's more of a gritty outdoor multiplex doing bulk business in a seedy neighborhood. By day, it's a parking lot lined with stalls for the huge Swap Shop flea market, which offers both an on-site McDonald's and the Daily Circus. At night the space is cleared for cars and moviegoers at $4.00 a head.

The Thunderbird keeps adding screens—thirteen at the latest count. It is by all accounts the largest drive-in theater in the country, and probably in the world. This is true even though the place opened inauspiciously on November 22, 1963, the day John F. Kennedy was assassinated.

Even today, the Thunderbird is a little unbelievable, and unexpected for many tourists.

When Florida visitor John Savage was growing up in New Hampshire, he went to drive-in movies with his parents—everything from *The Great Escape* to *The Dirty Dozen*. On vacation in Fort Lauderdale, he decided to take his wife and four kids to an old-fashioned drive-in. They found the Thunderbird in the phone book.

"When we called and they started reading off the list of movies, we said, 'Oh, this can't be a drive-in,'" Savage says. "But it is."

From any one Thunderbird movie, you can glimpse the screens for three or four others. Free previews are fine, of course, but not at the wrong moment. When the dramatic *Black Hawk Down* debuted in 2002, it was hard not to be distracted by Britney Spears dancing around in her underwear for *Crossroads* on the next screen.

The Thunderbird Drive-In is at the Swap Shop flea market— you can't miss it—at 3121 West Sunrise Boulevard in Sunrise. Admission is $4.00 per person. For more information, call (954) 583–7733.

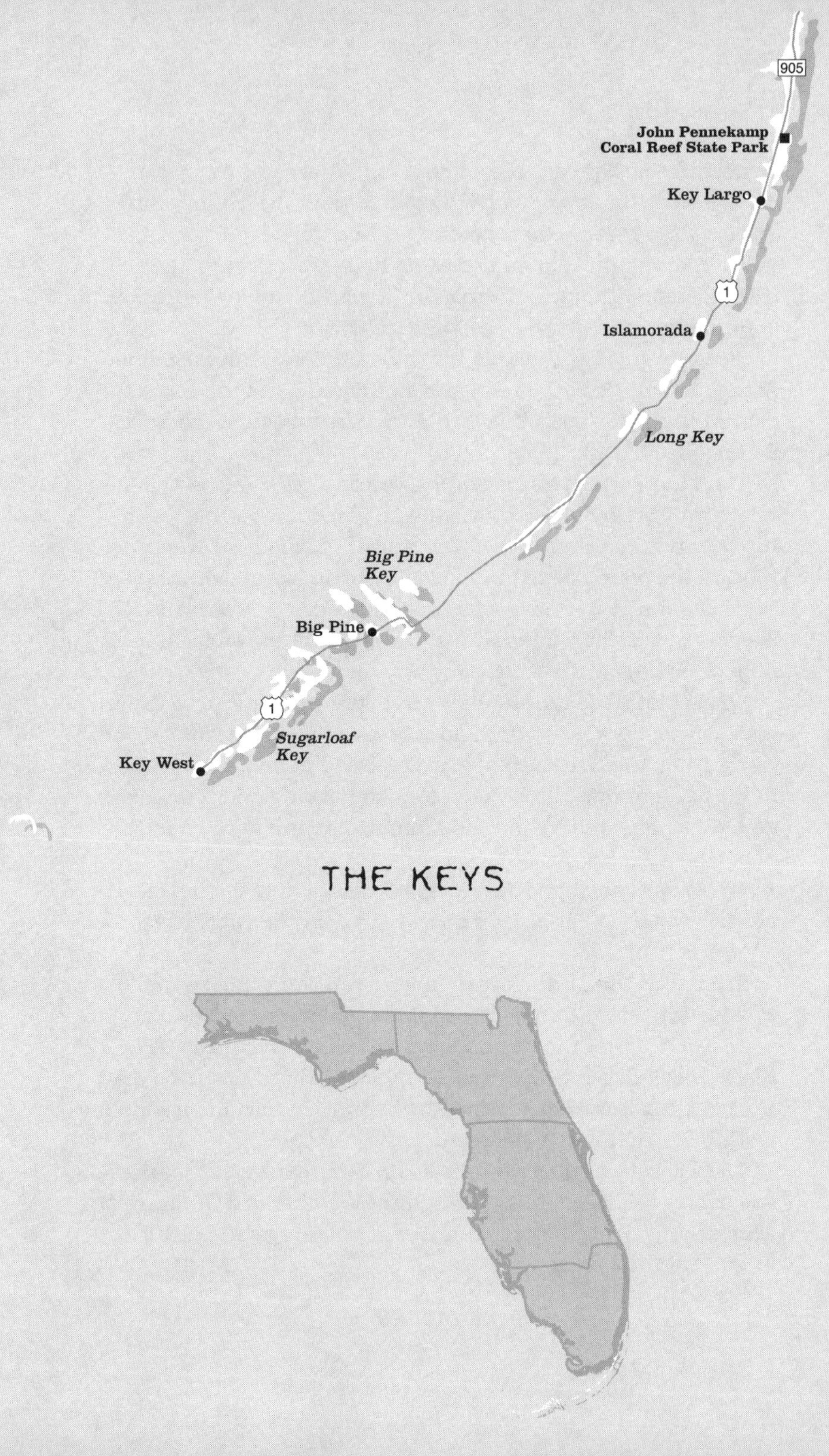

905

**John Pennekamp
Coral Reef State Park**

Key Largo

1

Islamorada

Long Key

*Big Pine
Key*

Big Pine

1

*Sugarloaf
Key*

Key West

THE KEYS

THE FLORIDA KEYS

ANOTHER MORTGAGE PAYMENT
Big Pine Key

Jannie Hohmann was looking for a way to separate her real estate company from the approximately 10,000 other real estate companies that do business in the Florida Keys. She decided to make fun of the fact that all real estate companies are basically the same, and named it Another Real Estate Company.

Oh, great. Another real estate company. Which, as it turns out, is exactly what Another Real Estate Company is.

Located on Big Pine Key, the office's sign is easily seen from US 1. Hohmann said her original idea was to come up with a name that would be first in the Yellow Pages. That didn't work out, so now she says the name is an attempt at humor. We think it's funny; whether customers will remains to be seen.

ROBBIE'S SCHOOL OF TARPON
Islamorada

R obbie's Marina in Islamorada sells bait and rents kayaks, but the main attraction swims beneath the docks. They're tarpon—big ones, and lots of them—and they school outside the marina like giant silver sardines. For anglers who know tarpon as fierce saltwater game fish, this is curious indeed—imagine a pride of lions lining up to be fed like a cuddle of kittens.

The story goes that an injured tarpon named Scarface was rehabilitated at Robbie's in 1976, and it kept returning to the dock. Soon there were dozens of tarpon, scores of them, all waiting to be fed. They show up in the morning and leave in the evening, unless there's really cold weather or really rough seas.

Some 50,000 people visit Robbie's each year; the more notable visitors have included tennis star Chris Evert and former Vice President Al Gore.

For $1.00, guests get a pail of herring—tiny ones—to feed to the tarpon. The huge fish mill around the docks and will even rise out of the water to grab a bite. Above the docks, it gets just as crowded.

"Oh, we're jammed all the time," said Joe Saba, a backcountry guide at Robbie's. "We opened at eight this morning, and I've already sold 200 pounds of bait."

Robbie's Marina is at mile marker 77 under the Lignumvitae Bridge in Islamorada. For more information, call (305) 664-9814.

THE NAME "TOURIST TRAP" MUST HAVE ALREADY BEEN TAKEN

*W*hy are the Florida Keys called the Keys? Don't blame Ponce de León, he of Fountain of Youth fame. The explorer, who apparently suffered from a much too vivid imagination, decided after seeing the chain of islands on the horizon for the first time that they looked like men who were suffering. (Remember, this was way before wives started dragging their husbands to gift shops.) He gave the islands the name "Los Martires," or "the martyrs."

Perhaps realizing that future chambers of commerce would have trouble warming up to the slogan "Be a Martyr! Visit Martyr West!," the chain was eventually renamed "keys" from the Spanish *cayos,* meaning "small islands."

So today we have Key Largo and Marathon Key and Big Pine Key, but no Martyr Key. Which is probably a good thing.

UNDERSEA LODGING, A LA JULES VERNE
Key Largo

The Jules Verne–inspired Undersea Lodge may be the only underwater hotel in the world, but it's hardly *20,000 Leagues Under the Sea.* The submersible doesn't move, and there's no mad captain bent on taking over the world. As a former NASA research vessel, it's more science fact than fiction.

Then again, the place was featured on the old television show *Lifestyles of the Rich and Famous,* and host Robin Leach could be pretty frightening.

The unique lodge, which opened in 1986, is a mere 21 feet beneath the surface of Emerald Lagoon in Key Largo. Guests pay more than $300 a night to dive into the hotel, entering through a wet room before enjoying two bedrooms, a bathroom, and a living room, along with huge round windows that offer a stunning view of surrounding marine life.

Talk about sleeping with the fishes.

The Undersea Lodge isn't exactly spacious, or luxurious, but it does offer some amenities. These include hot showers, air-conditioning, and televisions with VCRs. If guests order the lodge luxury package, a "mer-chef" will see to a gourmet meal. For more casual meals, there's underwater delivery from a local pizza shop.

The lodge is filled with compressed air, and a soft bubbling sound is said to offer a fine night's sleep—if guests aren't suffering from Jules Vernian nightmares.

Those round lodge windows, some 42 inches in diameter, feature parading schools of angelfish and parrot fish, along with less colorful but more exciting barracuda. NASA originally used the laboratory vessel, known as *La Chalupa*—really, no kidding—off the continental shelf near Puerto Rico. The idea was to explore the similarities and differences between life underwater and life in outer space.

Guests today can explore the area around the lodge without heavy diving equipment. Instead, they use 100-foot "hookah" breathing lines left over from the days of research. Nearby is Marine Lab, an underwater facility devoted to research and education, along with a re-creation of a Spanish galleon wreck. The lodge offers hours of what is called habitat saturation diving, but guests don't have to have any scuba experience at all.

Jules Verne offers a three-hour class to acquaint noncertified divers with the equipment and procedures necessary to descend to the lodge, accompanied by diving instructors.

The lodge is monitored by a command center at the edge of the lagoon. An umbilical cable provides fresh air, drinking water, electricity, and telephone lines. Two couples or a group of six friends may share the lodge, but there are honeymoon packages available. Celebrity guests have included former Canadian Prime Minister Pierre Trudeau and Steven Tyler of the rock band Aerosmith.

Jules' Undersea Lodge is at Key Largo Undersea Park, 51 Shoreland Drive, Key Largo 33037. For more information, visit www.jul.com or call (305) 451-2353.

UNDERWATER PARK AND CHRIST OF THE DEEP
Key Largo

For a mainland visitor to the Florida Keys, it's hard to say which is more impressive, the colors of the coral reefs along Key Largo or the clarity of the water surrounding them. On a clear day, it's like swimming through an enormous saltwater aquarium.

Rainbow parrot fish dart about in brilliant purple and teal. Vivid green moray eels lurk along the bottom. Bright blue

KEY WEST OR BUST!

*I*f you look to the west of the beautiful Seven Mile Bridge, which connects Marathon and Little Duck Keys, you will see what looks like an ultralong fishing pier.

Besides the fishermen, there are bicyclists, joggers, walkers, and people just out to enjoy the view. What they may not be aware of as they gaze over the turquoise Gulf of Mexico is that they are standing on all that's left of the Eighth Wonder of the World, or Flagler's Folly, as it was referred to by less charitable sorts.

Henry Flagler, an oil baron and railroad tycoon (he built the first railroad connecting Jacksonville to Miami, which explains why there is a county in northeast Florida named after him), decided in 1904, at the age of seventy-five, that he wanted to build a railroad connecting Miami to Key West. Some say he wanted to do business with Cuba, only 90 miles to the south. Others say the fortune he amassed from Standard Oil left him feeling guilty and he wanted to give something back to the people. (We tend to go with the first explanation.)

No matter the reason behind it, the fact that there ever was such a thing as the Overseas Railroad is, to say the least, remarkable. The northern part of the railroad, from Homestead to Key Largo, had to be built in the Everglades, where heavy machinery sank in the muck. Between the mosquitoes, the snakes, and the alligators, few workers stayed on the job long.

The railway, which was more than 100 miles long, ran along 20 miles of man-made causeways and over 12 miles of bridges, of which the Seven Mile Bridge was the longest. The engineering challenges would have been immense even without the two hurricanes that barreled through the Keys during construction, resulting in loss of life, major equipment damage, and second thoughts about whether the whole project was worth it.

But Flagler, his health failing, never gave up, and kept pouring money into the project. "Go to Key West!" he exhorted his engineers after every setback.

The railroad finally opened for business on January 22, 1912. Henry Flagler rode the first train from Miami to Key West, where he was joyously welcomed by the 17,000 residents of the island that the day before had been accessible only by boat. New Yorkers could now board a Pullman in Penn Station and not get out until they hit Havana. (The Pullmans were loaded onto ferries in Key West for the 90-mile trip to Cuba.)

The Overseas Railroad didn't just cater to swells, however. A round-trip ticket from Miami to Key West cost $4.75. If you could wait until Sunday, the ticket price was only $2.50.

But as wondrous as it was, the Overseas Railroad never made a profit. What the Great Depression started, the Labor Day hurricane of 1935 finished. The most violent storm in American history, the hurricane's 250-miles per hour wind gusts and 18-foot storm surge irreparably damaged the railroad, and Flagler sold what was left to the state of Florida.

Three years later, the railroad reopened as a two-lane highway, the remnants of which are what you're really looking at from the new bridge. The tracks were torn up and fashioned into guardrails. With each lane only about 5 feet wide, truck drivers were instructed at the beginning of Seven Mile Bridge to pull their outside mirrors in to avoid clipping oncoming vehicles.

What if you broke down on your way to Key West and needed to pull off on the shoulder? Plenty of room: To the right was the Gulf of Mexico and to the left was the Atlantic Ocean.

Finding a mechanic on the bottom of the sea, however, was another matter.

Stop at Pigeon Key, mile marker 47, for a good view of the old Overseas Railroad. The key was once a camp for railroad workers. A visitor center on the east side of the island is a good place to learn more about the history of Flagler's Folly.

tangs join elegant angelfish and schools of French grunts, all
yellow and striped. In less than an hour, you'll see more kinds
of tropical fish than you can count, along with plenty of barracuda and sharks. Then there's all the coral: brain coral and
staghorn coral, pillar coral and ribbon coral, ivory tube coral
and orange tube coral. Finally, if you're lucky, a huge spotted
eagle ray, some 7 feet across, will glide along the bottom with
effortless grace.

It's small wonder, then, that this area is protected as both
the Florida Keys National Marine Sanctuary and John Pennekamp Coral Reef State Park.

The Key Largo coral reefs are remarkable for being both
beautiful and accessible. One of their most appealing attributes
doesn't seem that important until visitors arrive in Key Largo:
They're shallow. Many of the reefs are only 5, 10, or 20 feet
below the surface. This means snorkelers can enjoy them just
as much as scuba divers can.

"In some parts of the world, reefs are more of a diver's
thing," says Danny Jones, manager of state park. "Novice
snorkelers can go to any of the reefs around here."

Often snorkeling is less of a sport than a leisure activity.
With swim fins and an inflatable dive vest to keep you afloat,
hardly any effort is required. "If you're jetting around, you'll
scare the marine life, anyway," says Nestor Morales, a dive
master out of Biscayne National Park. "I tell people, 'The
slower you go, the more you'll see. Take it easy out there.'"

Looming over the reef known as Dry Rocks is the *Christ of
the Deep* statue. It's a 9-foot high, 4,000-pound bronze piece,
built in 1961, that was modeled after *Il Christo Degli Abissi,*
"Christ of the Abysses," near Genoa, Italy. Divers who happen
to be atheists don't care for the statue, and have protested
against it, but it's become part of the local seascape.

Even though snorkelers swim among eels, barracudas, and
nurse sharks, incidents and injuries are rare. They're much
more likely to get sunburned or dehydrated. The danger people
pose to the reefs, however, is very real. It takes hundreds of

years for a piece of coral to grow, but a careless or thoughtless snorkeler can snap off a piece in a second.

"It's a hands-off environment," Morales says. "There's a saying: Don't touch it, don't take it, don't break it." Reefs can get crowded, but the human impact on the coral is slight so long as swimmers keep their hands and fins to themselves.

There are many private tour and dive boat operators in the Florida Keys. John Pennekamp Coral Reef State Park offers dive, snorkel, and glass-bottom boat tours out of Key Largo. Call (305) 451–1621 for information. To the north, Biscayne National Park offers snorkeling trips out of Homestead. Call (305) 230–1100 for information.

A FAREWELL TO SAVINGS
Key West

One of Ernest Hemingway's wives (we can't remember which one; he had four) thought she would surprise the famous author by building him a swimming pool, the first on Key West.

There were only about a hundred things wrong with the idea, the most obvious of which were (1) Key West is basically a big chunk of coral, meaning workers had to chisel the 10-foot-deep pool by hand; (2) The Atlantic Ocean and/or Gulf of Mexico is available for swimming purposes about two blocks away; and (3) It was built in 1938 during the Great Depression, when money was scarce. The other ninety-seven reasons? It cost $20,000.

Hemingway was less than thrilled by the gift. In fact, he took a penny from his pocket and announced jokingly (ha-ha!) to his wife, "Here, take the last penny I've got!"

Papa then pressed the penny into wet cement near the pool, where it remains to this day. (The pool is behind the Hemingway House and is part of the tour.)

The Ernest Hemingway Home & Museum is located at 907 Whitehead Street, Key West, and is open 365 days a year from 9:00 A.M. to 5:00 P.M. Phone (305) 294–1136. On line at www.hemingwayhome.com.

THE END OF THE LINE
Key West

It's ironic that one of the things that makes Key West so popular is the fact that it's so remote.

It's almost 800 miles from Pensacola, in the Panhandle, to Key West. Miami may look close on the map, but you've still got a lot of driving to do.

Over time, Key Westers, or Conchs *(pronounced CONK)* as they prefer to be called, have hosted pirates, presidents, authors, playwrights, hippies, artists, the military, real estate speculators, and tourists. A Conch either learns to be tolerant or he moves someplace else.

In the 1980s, the Navy was threatening to pull out of Key West. The mayor, in a stunt intended to show how close Communist Cuba was to his city, water-skied the 90 miles to Havana in a little les than six hours. Nobody in Key West thought this was the least bit strange, and the Navy stayed put.

In 1982, Key West threatened to secede from the United States. The locals intended to call themselves the Conch Republic. Yes, plenty of alcohol is consumed in Key West.

Today, tourists try to capture the cachet of the place by visiting Sloppy Joe's Saloon on Duval Street, a favorite hangout of Ernest Hemingway when he lived here from 1931 to 1961.

They also have their picture taken by a thermos-bottle-shaped thing at the corner of South Street and Whitehead Street that marks the southernmost point in the continental United States. There's a painting of a conch shell at the top that reminds everyone that this is the Conch Republic; at the bottom, more lettering describes Key West as the "Home of the Sun Set."

Not nearly as ominous as the proximity of Havana, but, hey, it still makes a good picture.

HOLY JURASSIC PARK, BATMAN! IT'S A POLYDACTYL!
Key West

It's rather sad that the first question people ask when they take the tour of the house of Ernest Hemingway, arguably America's most famous author, is, "Where are the six-toed cats?"

They don't want to know what inspired *To Have and Have Not,* where he wrote *For Whom the Bell Tolls,* or who the old man was in *The Old Man and the Sea.* What they want to know is where they can find the felines with the extra digits.

You don't have to look far. Of the sixty-one cats on the property, thirty-four are polydactyl, meaning they have more than the usual number of fingers or toes. (Since cats don't have fingers, we are talking, in this case, about toes.) Most have six toes, but four of the cats have seven. They don't seem to behave any differently from cats with the usual number of digits, although a few of them probably get tired of being gaped at by tourists.

Cats with extra toes were considered quite valuable in the old days, and Hemingway obtained his first polydactyl cat from a sea captain. Its name was Snowball. (The cat's, not the sea captain's.)

*Posing for pictures is all in a day's work for the six-toed cats
at Ernest Hemingway's house in Key West.*

The cats did what cats are wont to do, and pretty soon the
Hemingway property was awash (aspray?) with polydactyl kit-
ties. Hemingway, for some reason known only to him, named
his mutant cats after celebrities and movie stars. There was a
cat named Bette Davis, one named Frank Sinatra, and another
named Marilyn Monroe.

Our tour guide, Mark, said the genetic integrity of the seven
generations of six-toed cats will never be in danger due to the
territorial nature of the beasts. If a five-toed interloper hops the
fence in hopes of contaminating the gene pool, he quickly
encounters sixty-one Hemingway cats with other ideas.

It's all very interesting, we suppose, if you like cats, but we
find the prospect of buying eighty pounds of cat food a week
poly-ridiculous.

The Ernest Hemingway House and Museum is located at 907 Whitehead Street. Phone (305) 294–1136 or contact the Web site at www.hemingwayhome.com. Admission is charged. The house is open 365 days a year.

THE SUN ALSO RISES, BUT IT ALSO SETS TOO
Key West

Key West was once a haven for pirates. Over time, it began attracting drifters, gypsies, hippies, real estate speculators, and tourists.

The jury is still out on whether any of this is an improvement.

In any event, the one thing everyone has in common is an appreciation of Key West's gorgeous sunsets. In other parts of America, people might just look at the sky and say, "My, what a lovely sunset." But this is, after all, Key West, and any occasion, even the daily setting of the sun, is reason for a party.

The party takes place every evening (sun permitting) at Mallory Square, at the foot of Duval Street. Legend has it that the famous playwright Tennessee Williams, gin and tonic firmly in hand, initiated the tradition of applauding the setting sun. By the 1960s, the tradition had a name: Sunset Celebration. Certain people were of the opinion that if a gin and tonic was good, LSD must be better, and they gathered at the square to watch Atlantis rising out of the clouds at sunset.

Today the scene is bizarre enough without hallucinogens. The setting sun competes for the crowd's attention with street vendors, jugglers, sword swallowers, contortionists, magicians, musicians, acrobats, and maybe even the Ghost of Atlantis if atmospheric conditions are just right.

The party begins about two hours before sunset. Just follow the crowd.

A GASTROPOD BY ANY OTHER NAME

*I*t is not unreasonable to ask why residents of Key West wish to be referred to as a marine snail.

A conch (pronounced conk) is a type of whelk, the Queen Conch, and also a lifelong resident of Key West. (A bartender informed us that people who have lived in Key West a minimum of seven years now qualify as conchs. Standards continue to deteriorate.)

Why conchs? Well, they are, or were, a staple of a Key Wester's diet. The chewy meat is/was eaten raw (ugh!) or marinated in vinegar for salad. Conch is fried to make conch steak, diced to make conch fritters, or stewed as part of conch chowder (yum!).

Conchs (the sea-critter variety) were eventually overharvested to the point that all Florida conch meat now comes from the Bahamas. That is fitting because some say the first conchs (the human variety) were British sympathizers during Revolutionary War days who hid in the Bahamas after announcing that they'd rather go to war than eat conch. (Many tourists, upon tasting rubbery conch meat for the first time, have made the same vow.) When Florida became a territory of the United States in 1821, Bahamians involved in the salvage industry moved to the Keys and brought the conch label with them.

Another theory suggests that conchs are called conchs because they used to eat a lot of the once prolific critters and used the empty shells as signaling trumpets.

Whatever the origin of the word, it is considered a good thing to be a conch. In the old days, families would put a conch shell on a stick to announce the birth of a baby. Today, city officials declare someone an "official conch" if he or she does something praiseworthy of a civic nature, and new residents are referred to as "fresh-water conchs."

Derived from the Greek word meaning "shell," the conch's Latin name is Strombus gigas. This, thankfully, is not a well-known fact, which explains why the Key West tourist conveyance is called the Conch Train, Key West High School sports teams are referred to as the Fighting Conchs, and the cheerleading squad is called the Conchettes.

"Go fighting Strombus gigas!" would simply not do as a school cheer, particularly on third and long.

THE OLD MAN AND THE URINAL

*S*ix-toed cats may or not be your thing, but there are other reasons to visit Ernest Hemingway's house.

Take urinals, for instance.

Papa Hemingway spent a lot of time in Sloppy Joe's Saloon on Duval Street. Tourists flock there to this day, hoping that the consumption of sufficient quantities of margaritas will inspire them to write the Great American Novel. (America is still waiting.)

Anyway, Hemingway and the urinal in Sloppy Joe's men's room formed a relationship, of sorts, to the point that when Hemingway bought his house on Whitehead Street, he decided to bring the bathroom fixture along with him.

Today the urinal serves as a drinking fountain for the home's sixty-one cats. None of them, to our knowledge, has written the Great American Novel either.

DIARY OF A HURRICANE
Long Key

The so-called Labor Day hurricane of 1935 has the dubious distinction of being the most violent storm in American history.

With sustained winds of 200 miles per hour and gusts possibly exceeding 250 miles per hour (exact numbers are unavailable because all wind-measuring equipment was destroyed), the Labor Day hurricane killed 423 people in the Keys: 164 civilians and 259 World War I veterans staying in work camps while building US 1. Most victims drowned when an 18-foot wall of water surged over the low-lying Keys. Some were killed by flying debris; some were simply sandblasted to death.

J. E. Duane, an observer for the Weather Bureau, was in charge of a fishing camp on Long Key when the eye of the brutal Category 5 hurricane passed around 9:30 P.M. on September 2, 1935. Here is his account:

September 2:

2 P.M. *Barometer falling; heavy sea swell and a high tide; heavy rain squalls continued. Wind from N. or NNE., force 6.*

3 P.M. *Ocean swells have changed; this change noted was that large waves were rolling in from SE., somewhat against winds which were still in N. or NE.*

4 P.M. *Wind still N., increasing to force 9. Barometer dropping 0.01 every five minutes. Rain continued.*

5 P.M. *Wind N., hurricane force. Swells from SE.*

6 P.M. *Barometer 28.04; still falling. Heavy rains. Wind still N.*

6:45 P.M. Barometer 27.90. Wind backing to NW., increasing; plenty of flying timbers and heavy timber, too—seemed it made no difference as to weight and size. A beam 6 by 8 inches, about 18 feet long, was blown from north side of camp, about 300 yards, through observer's house, wrecking it and nearly striking 3 persons. Water 3 feet deep from top of railroad grade, or about 16 feet.

7 P.M. We are now located in main lodge building of camp; flying timbers have now begun to wreck this lodge, and it is shaking on every blast. Water has now reached level of railway on north side of camp.

9 P.M. No signs of storm letting up. Barometer still falling very fast.

9:20 P.M. Barometer 27.22 inches; wind abated. We now hear other noises than the wind and know center of storm is over us. Heading now for last and only cottage that I think can or will stand the blow due to arrive shortly. All hands, 20 in number, gather in this cottage. During this lull the sky is clear to northward. Stars shining brightly and a very light breeze continues; no flat calm. About the middle of the lull, which lasted a timed 55 minutes, the sea began to lift up, it seemed, and rise very fast; this from ocean side of camp. I put my flashlight out on sea and could sea walls of water which seemed many feet high. I had to race fast to regain entrance to cottage, but water caught me waist-deep, although writer was only about 60 feet from doorway of cottage. Water lifted cottage from its foundations, and it floated.

10:10 P.M. The first blast from SSW., full force. House now breaking up—winds seems stronger than any time during storm. I glanced at the barometer which read 26.98 inches, dropped it in water and was blown outside to sea; got hung up in broken fronds of coconut tree and hung on for dear life. I was then struck by some object and knocked unconscious.

September 3:

2:25 P.M. I became conscious in tree and found I was lodged about 20 feet above ground. All water had disappeared from island; the cottage had been blown back on the island, from whence the sea receded and left it with all people safe.

Hurricane winds continued till 5 A.M. and during this period terrific lightning flashes were seen. After 5 A.M. strong gales continued throughout the day with heavy rain.

A stone monument to the victims of the 1935 Labor Day hurricane can be found on Islamorada at Mile Marker 82 on the oceanside. Called the Florida Keys Memorial, the monument is made of native keystone and bears a frieze depicting coconut palms bending in the hurricane winds while an angry sea laps at the bottom of their trunks. In 1937, the cremated remains of 300 victims were placed within the tiled crypt in front of the monument.

IF YOU BUILD IT, THEY WON'T NECESSARILY COME
Sugarloaf Key

Of all the batty ideas, this one has to be the battiest.

Richter Clyde Perky was one of the biggest landowners in the Florida Keys in the 1920s. He founded a town on Sugarloaf Key called, unimaginatively enough, Perky. The centerpiece of the town was a fancy fishing resort to which wealthy tourists from New York and other points north were transported aboard Henry Flagler's new Overseas Railroad to Key West.

The resort had everything a vacationer might want: a lodge, guest cottages, a restaurant, and a fully equipped marina. Unfortunately, it also had something every vacationer didn't want: swarms and swarms of relentless, blood-sucking mosquitoes.

South Florida was mosquito heaven in those days. Locals pretty much accepted them as a fact of life, but tourists were not so forgiving, and business at the lodge dried up faster than a Yankee in Bermuda shorts.

But Perky was not about to be beaten by a lowly insect. He began reading a book titled *Bats, Mosquitoes, and Dollars*. Bats, he learned, love to eat mosquitoes. Perky loved dollars. He learned to love bats.

After contacting the book's author, Dr. Charles A. R. Campbell, Perky began construction of a giant bat roost in March 1929. The 30-foot-high unpainted wooden tower was built behind what is now Sugarloaf Lodge at a cost of $10,000. The stubby, shingled pyramid with a louvered door to allow the bats in and out sits on four legs and looks a little like an unfinished wooden rocket ship waiting to take off.

Perky might as well have tried flying it to the moon, because the bat house never attracted a single bat.

This puzzled Perky, because he had seen bats flitting about Sugarloaf Key in the evening. Why were they turning up their noses at his house?

For answers, Perky again contacted Dr. Campbell. After some thought, Dr. Campbell decided what the bat tower needed was bat bait. What are the ingredients of bat bait? Oh, just everyday things you've probably got lying around the house. Things like bat guano and ground-up sex organs of female bats. Mix it all together and you have something that Perky's right-hand man, Fred L. Johnson, said smelled "like nothing on earth."

You would think that bats would come from miles around to wallow in something as aromatic as Dr. Campbell's special bat bait. But the bats of Sugarloaf Key were apparently fussier than most, and they continued to stay away in droves.

The Perky Bat House on Sugarloaf Key never solved the island's mosquito problem, but it sure did exude some out-of-this-world aromas.

Time passed. The bat bait, aged by heat and humidity, went from smelling like nothing on earth to smelling like nothing in the solar system or even nearby galaxies. Still no bats, although occasionally a passing bird would be knocked unconscious by the stink and fall from the sky. We're making that last part up. We think.

Today, the Perky Bat House is as batless as ever, but Monroe County Mosquito Control's insecticide sprays have, too late for Richter Clyde Perky, finally solved the problem of mosquitoes on Sugarloaf Key.

So the story has a happy ending, in a batty sort of way.

The Perky Bat House is located behind Sugarloaf Key Lodge at mile marker 17. Turn at the tennis courts, and it's down a dirt road about a quarter of a mile.

INDEX

ABOUT THE AUTHORS

David Grimes is a nationally syndicated humor columnist who works for the *Sarasota Herald-Tribune.* He has won many awards, include the coveted Tin Kazoo from the Venice Community Center and a rubber chicken from *Sarasota* magazine. David lives in Bradenton with his wife, Teri, his son, Michael, and two incontinent pugs.

Tom Becnel writes feature stories and an outdoor recreation column called Go! for the *Sarasota Herald-Tribune.* He lives in Port Charlotte with his wife, Naomi, and daughters Audrey and Marie—the Go! girls.